Chipping Norton: The Story of a Market Town

David Eddershaw first came to Chipping Norton as a history teacher in 1964 and later became Education Officer and Assistant Director of the County Museum Service. For many years he has enjoyed sharing his love of Oxfordshire history, and especially Chipping Norton's, through lecturing and writing. His other publications include *The Civil War in Oxfordshire*, Sutton 1995; *The Story of the Oxfordshire Yeomanry*, Oxon. Yeomanry Trust 1998; *Using Local History Sources – A Teacher's Guide* (with James Griffin), Hodder 1996; *The Street Names of Chipping Norton*, Chipping Norton Bookshop 1999; *A Country Brewery, Hook Norton 1849-1999*, Hook Norton Brewery Co. Ltd 1999.

Chipping Norton

The Story of a Market Town

David Eddershaw

POUNDSTONE PRESS

First published in 2006
by Poundstone Press
Jaffé & Neale
1, Middle Row, Chipping Norton
Oxfordshire OX7 5NH

ISBN-10 0955241006
ISBN-13 9780955241000

Contents

Acknowledgements

This book was originally conceived simply as another revised edition of the *History of Chipping Norton*, first written by Eileen Meades in 1949 and revised by her for a second edition in 1984. That book has remained the chief source of information for anyone interested in the town's history for over half a century and the starting point for all subsequent local historians, as it was for me. As work on revising it progressed, however, there was so much new material to add that it proved impossible to update her work while retaining the style of the original and so the attempt was abandoned and this new book is the result. Readers familiar with Meades' *History* will easily recognise similarities in some passages which have survived that process and I am very happy to acknowledge my debt to her. Specific quotations from the original are used with the permission of the copyright holder, the Centre for Oxfordshire Studies.

I could not have produced this book without the generous and expert assistance of three good friends and colleagues: Dr Adrienne Rosen of Oxford University Department for Continuing Education, Ralph Mann and Robert Evans, all of whom have made their research freely available to me. Adrienne's scholarly work on the ownership of the manor from the 14th century and on the circumstances surrounding the grant of the charter in the 17th century have been acknowledged where her text has been used, but she has helped with a great deal of other information and advice as well as reading and commenting helpfully on the first draft. Ralph has been investigating the history of Chipping Norton as long as I have and has sent me valuable notes on a whole range of topics many of which are incorporated throughout the text. The sections on non-conformist congregations, the Rev Edward Stone and Henry Parish among others owe a great deal to him. Robert Evans is another historian whose research has proved invaluable and has willingly assisted me, especially with additional information on the Bliss family business and the strike.

The members of the Chipping Norton Historical Research Group deserve a special mention for their work in transcribing a huge number of probate documents mainly from the 16th and 17th centuries, which have produced so much fascinating detail about life and death in that period, and again I have been able to draw freely on this material, the only regret being that space did not allow me to use more.

Chipping Norton Museum of Local History, as well as housing a growing collection of both documentary and three-dimensional material, has a considerable archive of old photographs. A number are reproduced with their permission and I am grateful to Pauline Watkins for so quickly finding the images I requested and making digital copies of them.

John Grantham kindly allowed me to use his corrected version of the only surviving copy of the Chipping Norton Enclosure map, without which no history of the town would be complete.

The cover illustration is from an engraving of about 1850 hand coloured and generously donated by Trevor and Valerie Perkins of Trada, picture framers and print sellers in Chipping Norton.

I am grateful also to Chipping Norton Town Council, Oxfordshire Record Office and the Centre for Oxfordshire Studies for permission to reproduce items in their ownership or collections.

I am especially grateful to James Griffin for many hours spent checking and correcting successive drafts of the text.

Chapter 1

The Origins of Chipping Norton

Eileen Meades' opening sentence in both the earlier editions of her *History of Chipping Norton* stated that 'the origin of Chipping Norton, like that of many ancient towns, is lost in the mists of the past'. While that is still largely true, more recent work by archaeologists and historians perhaps allows us to see through the mist a little further than was possible when she was writing. There is still little precise information about the first settlement on this site, but archaeological evidence now makes it possible to assert with some confidence that there was human activity close to the modern site of Chipping Norton in the late Neolithic, Bronze and Iron ages, and a Roman villa, perhaps associated with a shrine, by the third century AD.

It is tempting to look for some connection with the nearby Rollright Stones and the Neolithic 'Whispering Knights' burial chamber. The stone circle is thought to date from about 2500 –2000 BC in the Bronze Age, but while it was no doubt a monument of great social and religious importance it has been pointed out that its construction would not have required a very large labour force and it cannot be taken to imply extensive permanent settlements in the area. It is at the centre of a scatter rather than a large concentration of round barrows, which if there were more might be taken as indicators of a settlement. It stands in a prominent hilltop position next to a prehistoric trackway suggesting regular travel through the area, but not necessarily a settled local community of any size. The erection of such an important monument here may owe more to the appropriateness of the site than to density of local settlement. Closer to modern Chipping Norton, however, a significant scatter of worked flint fragments and tools have been picked up from fields east of the town, and these do suggest an occupied site where domestic chores like cooking and preparation of hides were taking place as well as the production of flint tools, though the flint itself must have been brought from elsewhere by

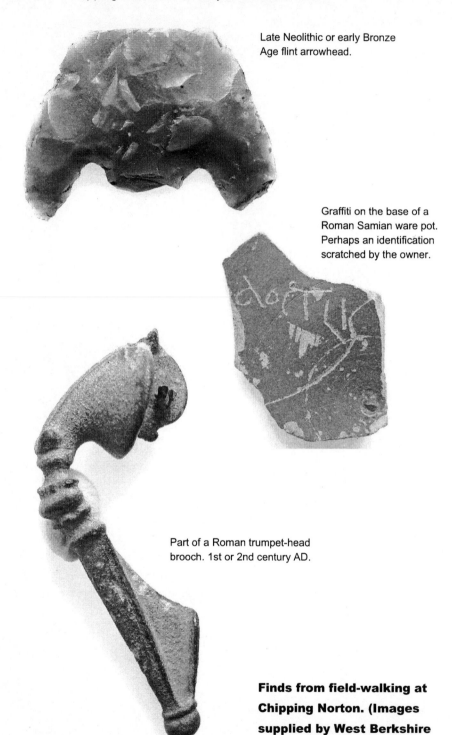

Late Neolithic or early Bronze Age flint arrowhead.

Graffiti on the base of a Roman Samian ware pot. Perhaps an identification scratched by the owner.

Part of a Roman trumpet-head brooch. 1st or 2nd century AD.

Finds from field-walking at Chipping Norton. (Images supplied by West Berkshire Archaeology Service.)

traders. Some of these flints suggest a presence as early as the Mesolithic period but most date from the Neolithic and Bronze Age, indicating that the site was used over a very long period.[1]

During the late Bronze and Iron Ages more extensive farming and settlement spread out from the river valleys into the upland areas of Oxfordshire and it is likely that forest clearance on the higher ground took place at this time. There was an Iron Age hill fort at Chastleton and by now a settlement near the Rollright Stones. A few miles to the south of Chipping Norton several sections of the earthwork known as Grim's Ditch might represent a fairly important concentration of the Dobunni tribe in whose territory the future site of Chipping Norton lay. A small investigation on the Primsdown industrial estate in 2005 discovered a probable prehistoric field boundary with animal bones and a single piece of mid to late Iron Age pottery, hinting at settled farming here.

When we come to the period of the Roman occupation the evidence for settlement at Chipping Norton is much stronger. Two major Roman roads were constructed only a few miles away soon after the invasion: Fosseway to the west and Akeman Street to the south. These linked important Roman towns and attracted development along their routes. Villas, which were probably the dwellings attached to large estates, have been discovered at places like Ditchley, Fawler, Shakenoak, North Leigh, Asthall, Great Tew, Wigginton and perhaps at Churchill Downs (where a Roman stone coffin from an important burial was also found in the 1980s). These suggest widespread exploitation of the land for farming so that it would be reasonable to expect some activity near Chipping Norton.

An impressive quantity of Roman coins, pottery and other artefacts have been picked up here over a long period. As long ago as the late eighteenth century the *Universal British Directory* made a passing comment about Chipping Norton that 'Roman coins are frequently found there'. A hundred years later a small hoard of coins was found on the William Fowler allotments behind Burford Terrace and others have been found at Oldner, in a garden on Burford Road, at Walterbush Farm, in the market place and near Station Road. These locations suggest a concentration on the high ground to the south-east of the present town and it is on private land in this general area that the most important finds have been made in recent times. A large number of coins has been picked up as a result of fieldwalking together with other small items like

---

1 A curious feature of some of these ancient flints is that a few of them are thought to show evidence of reworking as gun flints in modern times.

Carved stone head from the Roman site at Chipping Norton. Possibly representing the god Jupiter, it is thought to date from the late 2nd century. (Chipping Norton Museum.)

brooches and spoons.[2] Pottery sherds are very common and include some good quality Samian ware imported from the continent as well as colour-coated wares from the Oxfordshire, Nene Valley and New Forest potteries. In addition there is a quantity of fragments from more everyday items like cooking bowls, mortaria, beakers, and flagons, etc. Patches of light coloured mortar or wall plaster have shown up in the soil during ploughing and a small section of wall was uncovered close to the surface. Most significant of all was the discovery of a carved stone head, probably dating from the second half of the second century, turned up by ploughing in 1972. This represents the face of a god, possibly Jupiter, and is thought to have been a kind of plaque mounted on a wall, rather than a statue.

Although so many finds have been made through fieldwalking, only the general area of the finds has been recorded and as there has been no systematic excavation or other scientific survey of below ground features, it is impossible to build up an accurate plan of the site or to be sure of its extent. In spite of this it is clear that a site of some importance existed here in the Roman period. The carved stone head has prompted the theory that there was

2 I am indebted to Graham Cashmore for allowing me to see the finds which he has painstakingly collected over a number of years, and to Kate Sutton (Finds Liaison Officer for Oxon and Berks) for her analysis of them. They include both Roman material and the flints referred to earlier.

a local shrine or temple. There are several other examples in Oxfordshire. If there was one here it may have served a local community as many others did, or it could have been a more isolated place away from other settlements. In either case it could have provided a focus not only for worship at the shrine but also for other activities like trading. (It would be interesting indeed if there was a market or seasonal fair as early as the second century, close to the site of the later market town of Chipping Norton.) The great majority of the other finds, however, date from much later – the third and fourth centuries. They clearly indicate a high status dwelling, almost certainly a villa similar to others known to have existed in Oxfordshire. One can only speculate about the existence of an early shrine, perhaps even a Celtic one near the source of the local river and later assimilated into Roman religious practices, which may or may not have survived alongside the later villa built by some wealthy landowner exploiting the agricultural potential of the area at the height of the Roman occupation.

Whether this occupation site continued much after the collapse of Roman administration in Britain in AD 410 and developed into the Saxon village of Norton six hundred years later is quite impossible to say because there is so far a complete lack of local evidence during that long period. The 'mists of time' are pretty thick over this area and we can only discern a few faint hints. The local British population if it did survive, endured first invading bands of warriors and later settlers, mainly Saxons coming up the Thames and Middle-Angles through modern Warwickshire, and this may have been a thinly populated frontier area with vague and shifting political boundaries. The Hwicce to the west and north of Chipping Norton and the Gewisse to the south were later absorbed into the powerful kingdoms of Mercia and Wessex. It is noticeable today that several county boundaries originating in the late Saxon period meet not far from Chipping Norton and the boundary between the earlier Saxon dioceses of Dorchester and Worcester also ran here. Perhaps the Four-Shires Stone a few miles from Chipping Norton today hints at an uncomfortable period in the past when this was a border country disputed between powerful rivals.

Anglo-Saxon place names supply a few more clues. The Hwicce gave their name to Wychwood Forest. Their territory also extended as far as the salt mines of Droitwich and salt was such a valuable commodity for preserving and flavouring food that it was distributed over very long distances to other parts of the country. Of three known routes (saltways) through Oxfordshire two came into the north-west of the county from Gloucestershire, one going south towards Bampton and another passing very close to Chipping Norton at Salford ('salt ford') on its way to Rollright. The final clue is the name of Chipping Norton itself, which at this early period was simply Norton, a Saxon name meaning the northern 'ton' or settlement, perhaps a farm or estate. It is a common place-name similar to Sutton (south ton), Weston (west ton) and Aston (east ton). The implication of such a name is that it was to the north of somewhere more important, and in this case the most likely candidate seems to be Charlbury. An early text suggests that Saint Diurma was buried at Charlbury. He was an Irish missionary priest, one of the first to preach Christianity in pagan Mercia, and in 654 was consecrated bishop of Mercia. It is possible that in his lifetime he had established a minster church in Charlbury which would make it a regional centre with outlying estates to support it, of which Norton may have been one.

There is no evidence to tell us how this little settlement developed in the succeeding centuries or how it fared through the turbulent period of the Danish invasions and the battles fought by King Alfred to secure the survival of English Wessex. All that can be said is that by the time of the Norman Conquest the little village of Norton seems to have improved its fortunes and to have become important enough to be used soon after 1066 as the English headquarters of Ernulf de Hesdin, a high ranking follower of William I.

Chapter 2

The Manor of Norton and its Castle

The first time Norton is mentioned in any surviving document is in the Domesday Survey of 1086. By that time its inhabitants had survived twenty years of Norman rule as a consequence of Duke William of Normandy winning the battle of Hastings in 1066 and seizing the English crown. Winning the battle was one thing, but imposing his authority on the English people was more difficult. On Christmas Day 1066 he was crowned in Edward the Confessor's Abbey at Westminster, protected by his somewhat nervous soldiers in case any resentful English should cause trouble (they mistook the noise of cheering by crowds outside for an impending attack). In the spring of the following year he returned to Normandy, leaving his half-brother Bishop Odo of Bayeux in charge during his absence. While there he recruited a number of ambitious men to follow him back and help take possession of the newly conquered kingdom, promising them rich rewards in the form of lands confiscated from the English. Among them was a man called Ernulf from Hesdin, a small town in Flanders, the region from which William's own wife Matilda came.[1]

William clearly valued Ernulf's support and he was given charge of no less than eleven manors in various parts of England, one of which was Norton in Oxfordshire where the previous English lords Aluric and Ulward were expelled and Ernulf installed in their place. He also held land in Ledwell and Black Bourton, but it seems that he made his main residence at Norton, issuing a charter from here in the presence of the members of his household.

---

1 It is possible that Ernulf de Hesdin fought at Hastings rather than coming over later. Beryl Platts, *Origins of Heraldry* (London 1980) tentatively suggests that the banner of Hesdin may be identifiable on the Bayeux Tapestry among those of other Flemish knights.

The Normans, who were always a minority, imposed their rule on the English by force and the symbol of their power was the castle, a new sight in England and a stronghold from which a Norman lord could overawe his tenants or take refuge if attacked. The Anglo Saxon Chronicle complained of the Normans building castles all over England and oppressing the people. It was against this background that Ernulf de Hesdin probably erected the first castle in Norton, soon after 1066, no doubt forcing his new tenants to undertake the huge labour of digging earth out of the surrounding ditches and throwing up high banks to enclose the bailey.

Those ditches and banks can still be seen in the valley below the town, smaller now through erosion and the natural filling up of the ditches, but still impressive and still known as Castle Banks although the buildings have long since disappeared. It looks rather like the classic motte and bailey design favoured by the Normans all over the country. It seems inconceivable that the projecting spur of hillside which overlooks the banks (where the Victorian house called The Mount now stands) was not part of the plan, either from the start or at a later remodelling. The original structure was almost certainly wooden because the newly raised earth mound would need time to settle before it could support anything heavier, but stone buildings would have replaced it or been added to it at a later date, as suggested by the size of the foundations still forming visible humps in the grass surface. Because it was built into the slope of the hillside there could have been no water-filled moat, simply dry ditches at least on the upper side. Ernulf's castle was built in the valley because that is where the village was situated and its purpose was to overawe the inhabitants. That is also where the natural water supply is.

At some later stage it appears that Ernulf de Hesdin's castle was altered and enlarged, with further banks and perhaps more substantial buildings within its enclosures, resulting in the rather complicated plan to be seen today. It is possible that the first plan was a simple motte and bailey consisting of the two enclosures at the north end of the site. Perhaps a new improved castle was then built slightly higher and further south, using the spur (now The Mount) as a natural motte with a bailey partly overlapping that of the first castle. The most likely date for this is the 1130s at the time of the civil war between Stephen and Matilda. Because its then owner, William Fitzalan, had supported Matilda his castle at Norton was not one of those ordered to be destroyed when her son became king as Henry II.

Other later features of the castle site are the fish ponds. The main one now known as Pool Meadow is a very large rectangular enclosure artificially constructed and surrounded by low banks to contain the water flowing in at

Air photograph of castle site showing earth banks and impressions of internal structures. The house to the left of the picture stands on a mound which was probably also part of the castle. (Chipping Norton Museum)

the north end and back into the stream at the south. It is possible that others existed in what is now the garden of The Mount and that the field to the north of Pool Meadow, separated from it by a raised causeway, may also have been flooded. Fish ponds had an economic value in medieval times providing a supply of fresh fish for the households of their wealthy owners, and because they could only be constructed and owned by wealthy people they also had a high status value. The Pool Meadow fish pond would have been kept well stocked to supply the lord's table, but it is possible that other ponds were more for aesthetic enjoyment, a *plaisance* such as is thought to have been created at Deddington castle and elsewhere. The field name The Vinyards on the slope of the hillside facing the castle suggests that the lord was also supplied with his own grapes in the warmer climate existing in the thirteenth century.

The later history of the castle is undocumented. The Fitzalans, who became lords of the manor, may have lodged in their castle at Norton from time to time, but they soon inherited a grander one at Clun in Shropshire and eventually they succeeded to the Earldom of Arundel, so that Norton became a less significant possession. It is likely that a steward was appointed to manage the manor and he may have lived in part of the castle, but in time it became unused and derelict and was probably thought of as rather old-fashioned by subsequent lords who built themselves a manor house in the town. They may have re-used some of the stone from their abandoned castle and the rest probably went into the various extensions and rebuildings of the church. The last recorded reference to it is in a lease of the lands of the manor by Henry Compton to Edward Walford in 1566 which mentions 'the castell close ... whereupon was sometyme a castell standinge but nowe an old barne only, much in decaye.' The castle now only survives as an intriguing earthwork, a scheduled monument that awaits further investigation. A symbolic picture of a castle has been the image on the town seal since the seventeenth century.

The entry in Domesday book for Ernulf de Hesdin's lands in Oxfordshire includes this account of Norton in 1086 :

> The same Ernulf holds Norton. There are 15 hides and 1 virgate of land. Land for 21 ploughs. Now in demesne 10 ploughs and 15 serfs; And 22 villeins with 16 bordars have 11 ploughs. There are 3 mills rendering 62d (pence) and 60 acres of meadow. Pasture 1 league in length and breadth. It was worth 16 li (pounds); now it is worth 22 li. Ulward [Wit] and Aluric [Welp] held it.[2]

It is likely that the total area of the manor was similar to the ecclesiastical parish today (which includes Over Norton as well as Chipping Norton). It would have been divided into arable – 'land for 21 ploughs' – probably in two or three very large open fields, together with a large area of pasture for grazing livestock, and 60 acres of meadow for growing hay as winter fodder. Animals were also grazed on the stubble after harvest and on one of the fields which would have to be left uncultivated each year to allow this manuring to replenish it for the next crop. This open field system had developed in the Saxon period and was to last until the eighteenth century. At the time of Domesday all the land of the manor belonged to the lord and some of it was leased to tenants in return for labour services and payments in kind. The demesne represented the land retained by Ernulf, '10 ploughs' – almost half the arable in the manor. This was probably intermixed with that of his tenants, whose holdings consisted of long narrow strips scattered throughout the open fields. The villeins and bordars represented different levels of tenancy, bordars holding less land and having fewer rights. Serfs were the lord's personal servants without rights or land and completely dependent on him for their livelihood. There were also three water mills. These were valuable assets providing the lord with an income of 62 pence a year. It was usual for tenants to have to take their corn to be ground at the lord's mill and to pay for the priv-ilege. There is no indication of the location of these mills in 1086 but a later reference mentions a mill 'below the castle' and a very likely site would be

---

2 The names Wit and Welp have been added to the original text in another hand.

where the water leaves the Pool Meadow fishpond and falls several feet into the stream. Priory Mill in the part of the manor later given to Cold Norton Priory may have been another of the Domesday mills.

One other thing that can be said about the Domesday entry is that the value of the manor had increased noticeably since 1066. It was then valued at £16 but by 1086 it was worth £22, an increase of 40%. This may well be have been due to Ernulf's good management and exploitation of its resources. He had been described by one chronicler as a man remarkable for the skill with which he farmed his lands.

The villeins, bordars and serfs mentioned amount to 53 people and estimates of the population of the manor are based on the assumption that these represent heads of households only. There can be no certainty about what multiplier should be used to represent the rest of their family members but 5 is often used, giving a rough estimate for Norton of 265 people plus the occupants of the castle. The serfs may have been housed within the precincts of the castle itself and the rest of Ernulf's tenants would have lived in about 40 cottages probably clustered close to the church and castle, in the valley below the line of springs which later gave a name to Spring Street.

Ernulf and his wife Emmeline were probably devout people (their household included a priest), and it was apparently Emmeline who in 1081 gave the patronage of the church at Norton to the Abbey of Gloucester. The abbot appointed the rectors, and after 1328 vicars, when the abbey appropriated the income from great tithes for itself. Emmeline's gift confirms that although not mentioned in Domesday there was a church in Norton at this early date, though whether it was built by Ernulf or one of his Saxon predecessors is unknown. A blocked round arch in the west wall of the nave might be all that remains of it today.

Later in life Ernulf went on crusade to the Holy Land, perhaps in order to avoid brutal punishment for his part in a rebellion against William I, rather than from religious conviction. He probably met his death somewhere on this crusade. His eldest son, another Ernulf, also met an untimely death attempting to defend Shrewsbury castle against king Stephen in 1138. He and the entire garrison of 98 men were put to death when the castle was captured. His sister Avelina had married Alan FitzFleald and the manor of Norton passed to them and eventually to their son William Fitzalan, lord of Clun in Shropshire.

The manor of Norton was to remain in the hands of the Fitzalan family, with intermissions, until 1399. In 1181 it was subdivided through the foundation by William Fitzalan of the Priory of Cold Norton, the main buildings of which stood on the site of the present Priory Farm. Dedicated to St Mary,

St John the Evangelist and St Giles, it belonged to the Augustinian order. William Fitzalan endowed it with 'the manor of Over Norton and all the lands which he had around their houses, and all the land that he had in the field called Hyde towards Dunthrop, and all the land that he had in Retcumbe'.

In 1243 John Fitzalan succeeded to the Earldom of Arundel. Such increased status and power inevitably involved the family in the turbulent baronial politics of the time and in the 1326 Edmund Fitzalan was executed and his lands, including Chipping Norton, were held for a few years by Roger Mortimer. In 1330, however, they were returned to Edmund's son Richard.

Richard Fitzalan became one of the king's most successful military commanders both on land and sea, a diplomat and royal counsellor.[3] When he died in 1376 the manor of Chipping Norton passed to his eldest daughter Philippa, the wife of Sir Richard Sergeaux of Cornwall. Sir Richard and Philippa had three daughters, each of whom inherited a third of the manor, and for much of the fifteenth century these thirds were passed down through their families – the Pashleys of Kent and Sussex, the de Veres, earls of Oxford, and the Marneys of Essex and Buckinghamshire. The main estates of all these lords lay elsewhere, and they probably paid little attention to their property at Chipping Norton.

It was only in the 1470s that part of the manor was again acquired by a lord who was to play some part in local life. Richard Croft, a gentleman from Herefordshire, had been in the service of the future King Edward IV as a young man, and became a trusted official as keeper of the royal park at Woodstock and supervisor of building work at the palace there. In 1474 he was granted the third of Chipping Norton manor formerly held by John Pashley, and within a few years he acquired more property in the town and had to request the king's pardon for offences committed in the process. Richard Croft survived the struggle for power in Oxfordshire following the accession of Henry Tudor in 1485 and continued to play a prominent role in local government. He died in 1502, and asked to be buried in 'the chapell of Saint John Baptist in the church of Chepingnorton by the walle on the left syde of the said chapel ther where the cofer standith'. His tomb is still in the church today, although not where he requested.

Croft's son Hugh and son-in-law Sir John Rodney followed him as lords of Chipping Norton, until the manor was bought in the 1520s by one of the most powerful of Henry VIII's courtiers, Sir William Compton. Another third of

---

3 Information on the ownership of the manor from the fourteenth century has been newly researched by Dr Adrienne Rosen and it is largely her text that is included here.

Tomb of Richard Croft and his wife. Lord of Chipping Norton from 1474. When he died in 1502 he asked to be buried in 'the chapel of Saint John Baptist in the church of Chepingnorton by the walle on the left side of the said chapel ther where the coffer standith'.

the lordship, formerly held by the earls of Oxford, had been confiscated by the Crown in 1471 when the earl joined the Lancastrian campaign against Edward IV, and it was probably granted by Henry VIII to William Compton; the remaining third which had descended in the Marney family was later sold to Compton's grandson, bringing the manor together in single ownership once more. Sir William Compton had grown up at Court with Henry VIII and became his close companion. Gifts, lands and offices were showered upon him, including the post of Groom of the Stool with responsibility for the king's personal close-stool, giving him unrivalled access to the monarch. Compton amassed great wealth and a vast estate, then died suddenly of sweating sickness in 1528. The manor of Chipping Norton was passed down in the Compton family for the remainder of the sixteenth century, firstly to William's young son Peter, then to Peter's son Henry who was created Baron Compton in 1572, a rare honour from Elizabeth I, and then to Henry's son William who became earl of Northampton.

The Comptons had their own imposing country house at Compton Wynyates and like most of the medieval lords they had no need to live at

Chipping Norton, leaving local officials to collect their revenues from the manor court and the market and fairs. William Compton's will in the 1520s bequeathed twenty-six shillings and eightpence to his steward at Chipping Norton, Thomas Unton, and sixty shillings and eightpence to Robert Busby, his bailiff. Nevertheless there was a manor-house in the town in the early sixteenth century which was leased to tenants when not being used by the lord. The house stood in New Street, on the same site as the eighteenth-century mansion which later became the British School. It was a substantial building, described in 1566 as 'one messuage or dwellinge howse builte with stone standinge in the Towne of Chyppingnorton aforesaide with all the Courtes or yardes howses buildinges edefices barnes stables oute houses gardens and orchardes to the saide messuage or tenement belonginge'. Behind the house was 'one parcell of woodlandes called the Grove conteyninge by estimacion twentie and syxe acres'.

Chapter 3

From Village to Market Town

There can be little certainty about the shape of the village of Norton with its forty or so houses in the eleventh and twelfth centuries. The only sure points are the castle and the church, both near the foot of the sloping hillside, and the natural 'spring-line' a little higher up, where rainwater which has soaked into the ground at the top of the hill finds its way to the impervious layer of clay lower down and seeps out at this level all along the hillside. It is not unreasonable to assume that this was the main water supply and that most of the houses would have been on the lower slope of the hill from here down to the church. Perhaps the present Spring Street, Church Street and Church Lane suggest the layout of eleventh century Norton.

Even at that early date it is likely that cross-country routes between Burford and Banbury, and from London and Oxford to Stratford on Avon or Worcester passed through or near to Norton as they do today, although their precise lines may not have been quite the same as the modern roads.

Under the feudal system operating at this time the inhabitants of Norton, apart from serfs who were entirely dependent on the lord, supported themselves by farming land scattered throughout the open fields of the manor which they held from the lord as tenants. In return they were bound to work on his land for a number of days each week, with extra days at busy times like ploughing and harvest. They were also liable to make payments of produce at various times of the year and to taxes such as 'heriot', an entry fine of a man's best beast when he took over a tenancy. Such dues would have been enforced by the Manor Court and carefully recorded in its court rolls, though, sadly, none of these survive for Chipping Norton. Feudal dues and services were irksome to the more aspiring tenants, however, and the Hundred Rolls suggests that by 1279 the lord had agreed to accept a cash rent instead, amounting to 12s for a holding of thirty acres. Such an agreement was in keeping with the growing prosperity and independence of the inhabitants of a developing market town. Another landmark in the next century was the grant to the inhabitants by Richard Fitzalan in 1377 of a large area of common land. These were described as Smith Mead, the Sidlings of Primsdown as set out by the merestones (boundary markers), Vernhill on the north side of Primsdown, the Brue and Southcombe.

The absence of manorial records leaves only isolated mentions of local place names in other documents to throw light on the topography of the town. Meades mentions three deeds in the Bodleian library referring to mills and to 'a hill called Prenesdone' which is modern Primsdown. There was a 'middle mill', 'Sederysmille' and 'Newemille', a park enclosed with walls and a road or lane called 'Wodeweye' on the Chadlington side of the parish.

There is no surviving evidence of a charter for the borough at this date, either from the king or merely between the lord and his free tenants, as occurred in a number of other places, granting them the status and privileges of burgesses. However, it apparently sent representatives to a shiremoot at Oxford alongside other Oxfordshire towns and it is clear that by the beginning of the fourteenth century the town was being treated as a borough and Meades quotes a writ of 1346 addressed to 'the Bailiffs of Chepyng Norton' calling for three armed men for the king's army. Borough status was most clearly recognised by the entitlement to send members to Parliament, which Chipping Norton did in 1300, 1302 and 1353. The men chosen were John Mayhue and Robert de la Hurne in 1300 and Richard and William Aleyn in 1302. After 1377, perhaps at the request of the inhabitants who found it an expensive privilege because they had to pay their members' expenses, they were no longer required to send representatives.

Clearly, by the beginning of the fourteenth century the original manor of Norton had developed into a much more important and prosperous place under the stewardship of the Fitzalans. The key was undoubtedly William Fitzalan's success in obtaining a charter from king John in September 1204 authorising him to hold an annual fair in his manor.[1] Such fairs were usually associated with religious festivals and the charter for this one was for a four-day fair to be held on the feast of the Invention of the Holy Cross (3rd May) and the three following days, so that the first one would have opened on 3rd May, 1205. There had probably been a market of sorts for some time for the sale of local produce, but the fair brought a new level of trading to the town. Medieval fairs were essentially commercial occasions with an element of entertainment added on, drawing traders from a wider area and eventually attracting merchants buying and selling the famed Cotswold wool. Fitzalan was one of many lords who were establishing fairs and markets at this time with a view to increasing their income from tolls and fines associated with them – and the weekly market would undoubtedly have grown too with the success of the town's fair. Stall holders paid 'stallage' for their stalls and traders from other towns and villages paid a toll on all goods brought into the town for sale (burgesses of the town usually had the privilege of trading without toll). Trading often led to disputes and these were quickly dealt with by a special court (called 'pieds poudre' – dusty feet) which settled cases quickly within an hour. Officials were appointed to inspect weights and measures and the quality of goods being sold and to charge offenders, including those guilty of 'fore-stalling' (selling before the market bell) or 'regrating' (buying goods before it reached the market and then reselling it). The profits from all these sources went to the lord. The bigger and more successful the market or fair, the greater his income from it, hence the incentive to obtain a charter to establish this one.

It was probably William Fitzalan who laid out the huge new market place higher up the hillside from the old village, with space for sheep and cattle pens and all manner of stalls and sideshows. Around it he leased building plots to the more prosperous burgesses to encourage them to build houses and work-shops here, enclosing the market and creating a new town centre. The main roads may have been diverted to lead directly into it. The burgage plots were narrow so that as many as possible could be fitted in, and behind each was a long strip of land with a 'back lane' giving access to the rear. Thus the shape of the town was transformed by a conscious act of medieval town planning, taking on the shape it still retains today.

The buildings surrounding the market place have been replaced several times over the centuries but most of them still occupy the original narrow plots. Beneath 20 High Street is a relic of one of the earlier buildings, probably dating from the fifteenth century. The single room has a vaulted and groined ceiling and stone tracery in the windows, suggesting a high status building. In spite of having an external door and two windows it is now below street level, probably because of the inevitable build-up of the road surface over several centuries and the likelihood that it was originally built as a half-basement with an entrance via a flight of steps from the street.[2] The building above it may have been an inn or a wealthy merchant's house similar to other examples

---

1 For a transcription of the charter and a more detailed account of the Chipping Norton fairs see Ralph Mann's Chipping Norton Fair.

2 And possibly because the upper side of the market was purposely raised 'when the new road through the town was made in the seventeenth century' as Meades suggests. However, it is difficult to imagine why this might have been necessary and no docu-mentary evidence has been found.

Medieval basement beneath 20 High Street. It was probably built in the 15th century with a space in front of the windows and steps from the doorway leading up to the street. (Chipping Norton Museum)

found in Burford, Oxford and elsewhere.[3] The street names Upper Row (more recently 'Topside'), Middle Row and Nether Row or Lower Side probably date from soon after the creation of the new market place. Middle Row is almost certainly the result of encroachment by stallholders who found it worth paying a fine or quit rent for the convenience of leaving their stalls up between markets. These soon became permanent buildings. Such developments are typical of newly created market towns of the period.

The fair charter was renewed in 1253 for the benefit of William's son John Fitzalan, who was also granted the right to hold another fair on the last Friday in November. There seems to have been a third fair held around the feast of St Barnabas (11 June), granted in 1330 to Roger Mortimer, but its survival is

---

3 There has been much debate over the original nature of this room. Its groined ceiling, corbel heads and traceried windows have prompted the suggestion that it was a chapel, and it is marked as such on nineteenth-century OS maps. There is also a seventeenth-century will (William Turner, 1617) which mentions a house, almost certainly in the High Street, which has a room called 'the chapel chamber'. This reference was made less than a century after the Reformation and might have been based on actual memory, or it too could be just a supposition.

uncertain. Long before this, however, William Fitzalan's enterprise in obtaining the original fair charter and laying out a new market place had succeeded in making Norton the trading centre for the whole area, so well known for its markets and fairs that people began to call it 'Cheping Norton' – the place with the market. The name is first recorded in 1223.

Chapter 4

Church and Town in the Middle Ages

Many of the references to the town in the Middle Ages are in the form of records of wrongdoing, not because Chipping Norton was any less law-abiding than other towns, although Henry III's order in 1255 to the Sheriff of Oxfordshire to collect four marks from the town 'for many transgressions' might give that impression, but simply because these are the records that have survived. Disputes often led to violence towards property as well as people in the fourteenth century and in 1356 Thomas Neubold of Worcester complained that

> William le Spencer, chivaler, David le Flesshehewere of Chepyng Norton, Robert le Pope and Richard le Irish, [both of Chipping Norton] assaulted him at Worcester, trod down and consumed with cattle his crops and grass, felled his trees at Longedon, carried away the trees and other of his goods, assaulted his men and servants, and chased his tenants from the said town, and so threatened them that they dare not go to their own property to cultivate the lands and make his other profits there, whereby he has lost the service of his men and servants and the profits from his tenants there for a great time.

Robert le Pope perhaps came from the same Chipping Norton family as Hugh le Pope, who with his wife Matilda had been accused of murder in 1338. What sounds like a gang of highway thieves, containing rather surprisingly a fiddler and two clerks one of whom, Richard Stay, was a Chipping Norton man, were described in 1373 as 'common thieves and murderers and armed riders in the land of peace, as well as ambushers of the kings highways'. They were accused of robbing and killing two merchants at Hamptonesdowne and carrying out another robbery on the Fosseway near Cirencester where they stole two horses, cash and 'eight dozens of woollen cloth worth eight pounds', which suggests that they specialised in robbing

Cotswold wool merchants, no doubt attracted by the high value of their wool.

There was even an occasion when two high-ranking clergymen who both claimed to have been appointed rector of Chipping Norton came to blows, William of Cherington storming into the rectory and forcibly evicting Richard of Gloucester in 1293. In 1369 Roger de Horton, 'parson of the church of Chepingnorton' (as he was for thirty years from 1349 to 1379) found himself in the Fleet prison because he had failed to repay a debt of £20.

Occasionally people from Chipping Norton are recorded in more law-abiding circumstances, such as Thomas Smyth and another local man described as a 'worker with iron instruments' who were employed in the building of the new tower of Merton College chapel in Oxford between 1448 and 1450. From time to time men were appointed to collect taxes locally. These included John Shory, Thomas Wyssenden, William Aylton, John Ball the elder, Robert Raynold, and in 1446 John Stokes the elder.

These last two, Robert Raynold and John Stokes, were both named in 1450 as founder members of Chipping Norton's most important guild. To the medieval religious mind the concept of purgatory was very real, and this encouraged the growth of guilds, fraternities and chantries to offer masses for the dead in the hope of shortening the time spent in this necessary stage of purging. The endowment of a chantry involved bequeathing money or property to pay a priest who would say masses for the souls of the founder and his family, usually at an altar in a side aisle of the parish church. Particularly wealthy founders might have a special chapel built within the church. The earliest record of a chantry in Chipping Norton is that of St Mary endowed by Richard Wale at the altar of St James some time before 1290. By the time of the Reformation there were four such chantries in the church.

A mid-fourteenth century charter contains a reference to the 'Fraternitate de Chepyng Norton'. Fraternities and guilds were religious groups whose activities centred around the parish church but often had a social role outside it. Like chantries they too provided prayers for the souls of former members. Members raised money and left bequests in their wills for 'lights' (candles or tapers) to burn at the altar or near the statue of their saint. Wealthy guild members might leave larger sums or property to support the guild's activities or to employ a chantry priest. On the saint's feast day and at high festivals such as Corpus Christi, Easter and Christmas each guild would have its part to play in the ceremonies, processions and social activities surrounding the celebration. As well as their religious role within the church, larger guilds might erect a guild hall to serve as their meeting place and headquarters, endow almshouses or a school and provide other forms of charity for the poor.

Brass showing the wool merchant's mark of John Stokes. Brasses such as this were originally set in stone slabs on the floor of the church, but they were taken up in the 19th
century and parts of them remounted on wooden boards on the north wall.

Through bequests of money and property they sometimes amassed considerable wealth which supported their work as well as the feasts and pageants
which were commonly part of their social activities.

The Holy Trinity Guild, founded in 1450, included a number of Chipping
Norton's leading merchants and citizens and became an influential body in
the town. Its foundation document, dated 8th October 1450, provides clues to

its membership and activities. The licence authorised

> Nicholas Whitbill, vicar of the parish church of St Mary, Chepingnorton, John Yonge, John Stokes, John Huchyns and Robert Reynold, parishioners of that church, to found a gild of themselves and others, men and women, in the said church; and grant that the members have a perpetual succession and power to elect a warden or master yearly and to remove him. That the gild be called the gild of the Holy Trinity, Chepyngnorton, that the master and members be capable of acquiring lands and other possessions and of pleading and being impleaded in any court, and that they have a common seal and hold meetings and make ordinances. Licence also for the master and members to found a chantry of two chaplains to celebrate divine service daily in the said church at the altar of St Katherine and other altars thereof for the good estate of the king and queen, the said founders and members of the gild and for their souls after death and the souls of the king's progenitors; the chaplains to be appointed by the members and removed if need be. Licence also for the master and members to acquire in mortmain lands, rents and other possessions not held in chief, to the value of forty marks a year for the maintenance of the chaplains and of a fit person freely to instruct in the rudiments of grammar the poor boys and scholars coming to Chepyngnorton.

John Yonge, John Stokes and John Huchins were wool merchants and probably among the wealthiest people in the community. The vicar was included to signify the religious aspect of the guild and no doubt because of his standing in the parish, but the two chantry priests mentioned are 'to be appointed by the members and removed if need be', signifying the overriding authority of the lay members even over clergy. Interestingly the membership is to include both men and women and guilds were perhaps unusual in this inclusion of women as independent members. The warden or master was the chief officer of the guild and was elected annually. The guild was a legally constituted body with power to sue or be sued, to own property and even to hold land 'in mortmain', a privilege enjoyed by religious institutions excusing them from dues payable to an overlord. Not only did it intend to found its own chantry at the altar dedicated to St Katherine, but the two priests it employed would also say masses every day at the other altars in the church, thus benefiting the congregation at large and assisting the vicar in his work. Being loyal subjects, the guild would provide prayers for the king and queen as well as for guild members. Finally it would employ a 'fit person', almost certainly

Memorial brass of John and Isabell Young. He died in 1451, a year after becoming a founder member of the Holy Trinity Guild. Described as a 'woolman', his feet rest on sacks of wool – the source of his wealth.

another priest, to teach Latin to poor boys and scholars 'coming to Chepyngnorton', which seems to envisage boarders from outside the town. The Holy Trinity Guild clearly prospered. It founded a grammar school which survived until the nineteenth century and built a guildhall which is still in use today. At the time of the dissolution its chantry was the wealthiest of the four in the parish church, with plate weighing 46 ounces compared with the 10 ounces of two other chantries. This chantry chapel is thought to have been the one built between two of the pillars at the east end of the new nave, close to the chancel arch. Destroyed at the Reformation, traces of it were rediscovered in the nineteenth century.

William Fitzalan and his wife Avelina, some time between 1147 and 1158, had founded not just a chantry but a community of Augustinian canons which became known as Cold Norton Priory.[1] The Augustinians were highly regarded for their piety at this time and so were often selected to pray for the spiritual welfare of their benefactors in this world and the next. The priory was dedicated to St Mary, St John the Evangelist and St Giles. A twelfth-century seal found on a deed, shows a church with transepts, topped at each end by slender turrets, and a central tower with a pointed roof, which may simply be a stylized design or an actual depiction of the building. Closely connected with the priory was a hospital for the sick and aged, the only one in Oxfordshire mentioned in a list drawn up in about the year 1200. There was also a remote chapel 'the Chapel on the Heath' for the use of lay people and particularly travellers. Chapel House today stands on its site.

The priory was a small one and the value of its income from endowments is uncertain. In addition to the Fitzalan's initial gift of the Over Norton part of their manor, other bequests followed over the years from local people such as the grant of land in Chipping Norton in 'Stockwellestreet' by Richard Wine to the 'house of St John the Evangelist of Norton'. During the fourteenth century a dispute arose with the rector of Chipping Norton over the right to the tithes from this land, but in 1376 it was settled in favour of the priory, but with an annual payment of 5s to the rector. Among the more valuable endowments in the late fourteenth century were the Earl of Stafford's manor of Great Rollright and the advowson of Steeple Aston together with four acres of land, allowing the Priory to appropriate the income from tithes for itself while appointing a vicar to minister to the parish.[2] The canons exploited their land

---

1 Some information in this section is from work by Elizabeth Allen on the Brasenose College archives.

2 An expensive and beautiful medieval cope found in Steeple Aston church in the nineteenth century may be a further indication of the valuable gifts made to the Priory. Now in the Victoria and Albert Museum, it is a rare surviving example of Opus Anglicanum, the internationally renowned English embroidery using gold thread and precious stones. Cold Norton Priory owned the living of Steeple Aston, which possibly explains the presence of this cope.

holdings by keeping large flocks of sheep at a time when English wool was in great demand, as well as through arable farming to supply their own needs and for sale. In spite of this there were occasions when the Priory pleaded poverty, as in 1291 when it claimed that its income was only £16 a year and it was unable to contribute to a papal tax of that year. This might be the result of genuine reduction in income caused by some setback, like the sheep disease which was particularly widespread and damaging to flocks in the 1270s and 1280s, or it may merely reflect the general reluctance of English monasteries to pay taxes to Rome. On another occasion they complained of the 'intolerable crowds of wayfarers' demanding hospitality from them and stated that they were having difficulty finding tenants to cultivate their land, perhaps because of the Black Death. By the end of the fourteenth century it also appears that there was a degree of negligence and mismanagement and the prior, Robert de Enston, was forced to resign in 1396 because of his negligence and idleness 'whereby the priory is burdened with debt and short of vestments and books'. The bishop commented that he deserved punishment rather than honour but 'having compassion on his old age, he should eat at the prior's table unless a worthier person be present, in which case he must sit among the brethren. He is to attend all the services and shall be allowed one servant at the expense of the priory'. Things were no better ten years later when a further inquiry was ordered into 'the excesses and crimes of which there is public talk, especially the wasting of goods by the present prior and his contumacy.' Again there was a threat of dismissal but this prior, William Doddyngton, seems to have survived for another eleven years, finally resigning in 1417.

The last Prior of Cold Norton, John Wootton, died in 1496 and by 1507 the king had taken possession of the priory and its lands and buildings. It owned land in twenty-one parishes, possibly amounting to as much as 240 acres of arable, 3000 acres of pasture, 160 acres of meadow and 80 acres of woodland as well as 46 messuages and four mills. In 1512 the Bishop of Lincoln acquired them, having made an offer of 1150 marks, and in 1513 he gave the priory and its endowments to the recently founded Brasenose College at Oxford. For some years the priory buildings were used by the Principal and Fellows of the college as a frequent refuge from the plague when it was present in Oxford, while its rents supplemented the college income. Names like 'Chapel House', 'Brasenose Villas', 'College Place' and 'Priory Mill' are reminders of Cold Norton Priory today, as are the remains of a chain of fish ponds at Priory Farm, on the site of the priory, which would once have supplied the canons with fish during Lent and on the many other fast days in the medieval calendar.

The parish church of St Mary the Virgin. The exterior shows work of several different periods from the 14th to the 19th centuries.

Whatever the role of Cold Norton Priory locally, the centre of Chipping Norton's religious life was the parish church, originally said to have been dedicated to St Nicholas, then to St Thomas a Becket and finally to St Mary the Virgin. Like most churches it has been altered and enlarged several times, incorporating each new style of architecture in turn. Almost nothing remains of the Norman building but there are several examples of thirteenth and fourteenth-century work and its chief glory is the fifteenth-century 'Perpendicular' nave and clerestory with its soaring pillars and abundance of light (a style originally developed at the abbey church of Gloucester).

A number of alterations and additions were made in the fourteenth century. The chancel windows, the low stone screen which separates the chancel from the former Lady Chapel, the Decorated windows and the arcading and pillars between the two north aisles probably date from this period, as does the unusual hexagonal porch. (Only two other porches like this are known, one at Bristol and the other at Ludlow, which may have been known to the Fitzalans). Inside the porch are seats around the walls with lancet windows above and a groined roof with grotesque faces on the bosses, including a sheep. Above this is an upper room. Evidence of pre-Reformation features inside the church survives in the fragments of a chantry chapel in the

The impressive Perpendicular nave and clerestory in the parish church. A major rebuilding in the 15th century reflected the wealth and piety of local wool merchants.

nave, and the steps and doorway to the former rood loft, within the thickness of the same pillar, which was also rediscovered during the Victorian restoration. Rather unusually there are two north aisles. Perhaps the finest example of the Decorated style is the great window in the south aisle, with its elaborate stone tracery enclosing 98 separate areas of glass. Although this window fits well enough now, an earlier print of the exterior shows the top of it projecting above the roof. In spite of a tradition that this window was rescued from Bruerne Abbey at the dissolution and re-used here although it was too big for the space, it seems more likely on the evidence of former roof lines in the outer gable walls, that the roofs of both north and south aisles were lowered at the time the nave was rebuilt so that they would not obscure the new clerestory windows. Whatever the original reason, this roof has since been raised to accommodate the whole of the window properly. On the wall of the outer north aisle are a few of the brass memorials once set in stone slabs in the floor to commemorate some of the wealthier men and women of the town in the late middle ages. There were originally more, but a number were lost at the time of the Victorian restoration.

During the fifteenth century a major rebuilding was undertaken. This was indicative of the growing prosperity and civic pride of Chipping Norton and was similar to developments in other towns, especially in the Cotswolds and East Anglia where considerable wealth derived from the profits of wool and cloth was lavished on local churches. The whole of the nave was rebuilt in the Perpendicular style with tall pillars and panel tracery on the flat surfaces of the spandrels, and a spectacular range of clerestory windows under the heightened roof. The pillars are slender and the clerestory has more glass than stone in its construction: a very confident and skilful piece of building. Above the chancel arch is another fine window with a double layer of tracery. The accounts of the Prior of Worcester for 1447–48 record a donation of 3s 4d to the fabric of the church at Chipping Norton, hinting that the nave was being rebuilt at this time and perhaps suggesting a widespread appeal for funds. It has also been suggested that the form of the pillars in the arcade at Chipping Norton was based on the nave of Canterbury Cathedral and might be the work of the same master builder, John Smyth, or perhaps one of his masons. The result is one of the finest 'wool churches' in the region.

Chapter 5

Reformation and Rebellion

The early years of the sixteenth century may have seemed uneventful to the inhabitants of Chipping Norton. News would reach them from travellers along the roads through the town but most of them probably went about their daily business without much concern for national affairs.

This apparent tranquillity was soon to be shattered by developments following Henry VIII's quarrel with the pope and the subsequent breach with the Roman church. Papal authority over the Catholic church in England was quickly removed and the Act of Supremacy of 1534 made Henry its Supreme Head. These were not remote affairs that the people of Chipping Norton could ignore while getting on with their tranquil lives. Every male over 14 was forced to swear an oath accepting the consequent changes in the succession following the king's divorce. The next major step was the dissolution of the monasteries and seizure of their property by the king. There had been no monastery in Chipping Norton since the closure of Cold Norton Priory nearly thirty years before, but the news that others all over the land were being closed down and the monks and nuns dispersed must have been greeted with shocked amazement by most people in the town, although there would undoubtedly have been some who were glad to see it done. First to be closed were the smaller houses but they were soon followed by even the greatest, including well-known local institutions like Oseney Abbey in Oxford, Eynsham Abbey, or Chipping Norton's own patron St Peter's Abbey in Gloucester. Reactions to the Dissolution were strong enough in the north of England at least, to cause a major rebellion in 1536 'The Pilgrimage of Grace', and news of it would certainly have reached Oxfordshire, but it is not known what local opinion was in Chipping Norton at the time.

The real crisis for Chipping Norton came with the strongly Protestant reforms forced through after Henry's death by Protector Somerset in the name of the nine year-old Edward VI. Belief in purgatory and the consequent need for masses to be said for the souls of the dead was dismissed as mere super-

The remains of a former chantry chapel, probably that of the Holy Trinity Guild. Built in the 15th century, it was demolished at the Reformation soon after 1549. This fragment was rediscovered in the 19th century and incorporated into a new pulpit. Steps leading to the pre-Reformation rood loft can also be seen in the pillar behind it.

stition and this, together with the financial needs of the government, lead inevitably to an order in 1547 for the abolition of all religious guilds and chantries and the confiscation of their lands and possessions by the state. This was something that had a serious impact on ordinary people at the local level. The chantries in St Mary's church, set up by parishioners in earlier centuries and lovingly supported by subsequent generations, were swept away. The Report of the Chantry Commissioners in 1549 lists four chantries and estimated their income and the value of their property. The Chantry of Our Lady owned property and land worth £9 8s 4d a year[1] 'gyven by Master Lee to the maynteyninge of a priest to pray and synge for his soule and all Crysten soules for ever'. The current priest was sir Edward Holden, 'a man very well learned'. The chantry also owned plate which weighed ten ounces, perhaps a silver chalice or paten bequeathed like other property and land by past parishioners. The Chantry of St James had been endowed by Margaret Prynner and had an annual income of £7 6s 8d, plate weighing ten ounces and ornaments (such things as altar frontals, candlesticks or even jewels adorning a statue) valued at 6s 8d. Its priest was Robert Wheler, 'a man of honest behaviour and well learned'. Sir William Benson was the priest attached to the Chantry of St John founded by John Tanner and had a salary of £7 7s 4d; the plate weighed ten ounces and

---

1 This figure represents an estimate of annual income from rents.

ornaments were valued at 4s. The Trinity Guild was by far the richest and most important. It had for chantry priest the sixty year-old Sir William Bryan, also described as honest in his behaviour. He had a yearly salary of £6. The guild's charitable work included maintaining a school, of which Sir Hamlet Malban was schoolmaster with a yearly stipend of £6, and in addition providing alms to the poor amounting to £1 2s 9½d a year. The annual value of the property and land belonging to the guild was £16 15s 10d. The plate and jewels which were in the safe keeping of John Oppwood weighed about forty-six ounces and the ornaments were valued at 13s 4d. All of these chantries were closed down and their plate, ornaments and endowments seized.

The king's Commissioners who carried out the valuations, had power to provide for displaced chantry priests, to continue any customary payments to the poor and to allocate funds for guild schools to continue where they thought it justified. Thus they reported that the local inhabitants had made a strong case for the continuation of the Trinity Guild's school as there were many children in 'this great market town', so they agreed that the school could continue and Sir Hamlet Malban was allowed to continue as schoolmaster with a salary of £6 as before. In spite of similar petitions from other Oxfordshire towns like Banbury, Burford and Deddington, only Chipping Norton and Ewelme were allowed to retain their schools. The other former chantry priests were given pensions or found livings.

All this sounds very reasonable but it should not hide the devastating effect on the life of the parish of this and other acts and ordinances imposed by Somerset's government in a very short time. These included the banning of processions and banners, hugely popular features of parish life involving many people at the celebration of the great festivals and saints' days. Candles and lights in the church were also forbidden, except for two on the main altar. These had always been a special feature of otherwise dark church interiors, adding excitement to the glittering ornaments and gilded statues with their flickering smoky light, and the object of innumerable gifts and bequests in the wills of rich and poor alike either as demonstrations of piety or assurances of prayers after death. All images, statues, stained glass windows and the colourful paintings which adorned many of the walls in a medieval church were to be removed, including the great crucifix with its figures of Mary and John at the foot of the cross mounted on the 'rood beam' across the chancel arch, keeping this image ever before the eyes of the congregation. Symbols such as these had been so ingrained in the minds and weekly devotions of local people for generations that apart from a minority who already favoured the new Protestant teachings, the suddenness and authoritarian nature of the changes was very difficult to accept.

Another very unpopular aspect of the suppression of the guilds and chantries, like the monasteries before them, was that outsiders quickly stepped in to buy up their lands and property. Many local people, rich and poor, through their membership of guilds and fraternities had shared in the ownership and benefits of such property, and now it was being sold off to gentlemen to enlarge their private estates. Even the creation of a rabbit warren in the 1530s on former common land at Over Norton had provoked protests against Sir Walter Walsh who had enclosed it. Enclosure of common land was in any case deeply resented by those who lost their former rights, and Somerset himself had set up commissions to enquire into this evil, but little action had followed, so that local people had their hopes raised only to be frustrated by the inaction.

It was against this background that a serious rising took place in Oxfordshire, Buckinghamshire and other midland counties in the summer of 1549, perhaps sparked off by another government order that from Whit Sunday all churches must use a more Protestant form of worship contained in the new English prayer book. It was perhaps not any new doctrine contained in this book that upset people so much as the change of language – the age old Latin was replaced by an English version of the services and prayers, sweeping away the familiar and reassuring sound of the mass that had been part of the life of every parishioner from childhood to old age, whether or not they understood its literal meaning.

The Oxfordshire Rising coincided with two other major rebellions – the Prayer Book Rebellion in Devon and Cornwall and Kett's Rebellion in Norfolk and Suffolk, as well as numerous smaller outbursts across the country. Together they represented a major political and religious crisis for the government during the minority of Edward VI. Rebels from Buckinghamshire, Northamptonshire and Berkshire joined up with others in Oxfordshire and marched on Thame and Oxford. At Thame and nearby Rycote they attacked the property of Sir John Williams, killing his deer and some of his sheep, which they roasted and ate accompanied with wine looted from his cellars. Williams had grown rich through buying up monastic land and keeping huge flocks of sheep, and was thus an obvious target. At Oxford the Protestant scholar and reformer Peter Martyr, recently invited to England by Archbishop Cranmer and appointed Regius Professor of Divinity, was forced to flee for his life, and Magdalen College was singled out for attack, perhaps because of its deer park, which was plundered as a symbol of wealthy privilege.

The rebels then swept on to Woodstock, gathering reinforcements from other areas as they went, but here they got news that Somerset had ordered

Lord Grey of Wilton to go after them with a force of over a thousand German mercenary soldiers. These troops had been hired to deal with the rebellion in the West Country but the seriousness of the situation in Oxfordshire, and its closeness to the capital, made it urgent to deal with this first. Grey was a renowned soldier able to command the respect and support of the local gentry and his mercenaries were ruthless professionals with no sympathy for the local people or their grievances. It is possible that the Buckinghamshire rebels left at this point to return to their own county, but the remaining rebels moved north to Chipping Norton, where they formed a camp. Camps were a distinctive feature of all the major rebellions in 1549 and may suggest a degree of communication between rebels in different parts of the country. These events were often referred to as 'the camping time'. It was perhaps at this stage in the rebellion that several north Oxfordshire clergy began to play a leading part, including Henry Joys (or Joyce) the vicar of Chipping Norton. The main leader according to Grey was James Webbe, vicar of Barford St Michael, and the vicars of Deddington, Duns Tew, Bloxham and Combe were also implicated together with Henry Joys, prompting Somerset to describe the rebellion as 'a stir by instigation of sundry priests for these matters of religion', although it is clear that it had a wider social and economic basis than just religion. It was no doubt government policy to try to play down the scope and seriousness of the rising in this way. However, the camp at Chipping Norton was short-lived and ended in a tragic bloodbath.[2] On about the 18th July Grey's mercenaries attacked the rebels and easily defeated them. A brief and telling entry in the journal kept by the young King Edward succinctly describes the grim outcome: 'To Oxfordshire the Lord Grey of Wilton was sent with 1,500 horsemen and footmen, whose coming with the assembling of the gentry of the county so abashed the rebels that more than half of them ran their ways, and others that tarried were some slain, some taken and some hanged'.

The following day Grey assembled the gentry of the county at Witney and issued orders for the punishment of the leading rebels. Over 200 had been taken prisoner but most were subsequently pardoned. Those seen as ringleaders, however, were sentenced to particularly brutal and public deaths, clearly intended to deter others from opposing the government's reforms. James Webbe was singled out for trial in London, together with the leaders of the Norfolk rebellion, and was condemned to be hanged, drawn and quar-

---

2 Earlier suggestions that this battle took place at Enslow Bridge seem to be due to confusion with the much smaller rising in 1596, which did assemble at Enslow Bridge. More recent studies accept that the battle in 1549 was at Chipping Norton.

tered in Aylesbury, all of which suggests that he was considered the main leader. Ten laymen suffered the same fate including Thomas Bouldry a wealthy yeoman of Great Haseley who had led the attacks on Thame and Rycote. Henry Joys and the other vicars were sentenced to be hanged from the towers of their own parish churches. It was specifically ordered that all these hangings should take place on market days when as many people as possible would have to witness them, and afterwards the rebels' heads were to be cut off and displayed 'in the highest place for the more terror of the said evil people'. Charging the local gentry to see that the punishments were carried out, Lord Grey then left Oxfordshire and headed off to the West Country to deal with the rebels there. He reported to Somerset that 'the Oxfordshire Papists are at last reduced to order, many of them having been apprehended and some gibbeted and their heads fastened to the walls.' One can only imagine the trauma experienced by local people after these events.

It is possible that the gruesome sentence on Henry Joys was not carried out. It is known that the vicars of Bloxham and Duns Tew were pardoned, and although the Calendar of Patent rolls records the presentation of Edward Large to the parish of Chipping Norton 'void by the death of Henry Joys lately executed for high treason', the Oxford diocesan register attributes his death to natural causes. Appeasement had been one part of Somerset's strategy from the start and it is possible that the government may have been content simply to remove recalcitrant priests rather than turn them into martyrs.

The valuable property confiscated from guilds and chantries was soon sold off to raise cash for the government. Buyers were often speculators from outside the town who were likely to resell at profit quite soon afterwards. In 1549 John Dodyngton and William Warde, gentlemen, paid £1,675 4s 8d for the 'mansion of the late chauntry of St Mary ... and a garden adjacent to it in Church Lane, lately in the occupation of the incumbent'. One of the king's physicians, George Owen, received for the price of £1,098 12s 6d a grant of the 'house and garden in Church Street lately occupied by Robert Wheler, priest of the chantry of St James, together with the lands belonging to that chantry' and the house, orchards and gardens and two closes of land and pasture which had belonged to the late Chantry of St John. In December 1549 Edward Pese and William Wynlove, gentlemen, received a grant of

Four messuages, one garden, another messuage called le Gilde House and a yard and a half of land in the fields called Salford Feldes ... which belonged to the late Guild of Holy Trinity ... and a close and a little parcel of land in le Newstretende in tenure of Thomas Colton, a messuage, curtilage and garden next the tenement of John Tanner in

The Guildhall, showing the original central portion with later additions at each end.

tenure of John Kelmyngton, another messuage of garden in le Newestrete in tenure of Roger Cowper alias Lyttleford, a cottage and land in Estfelde and Westfelde in tenure of Thomas Fletcher, and 4½ acres of meadow in Brokemeade in tenure of Robert Halifax alias Crowder.

For these possessions of the late chantry of St Mary they paid to the crown the sum of £2,551 5s 10½d. Other chantry possessions in Newestrete, Churchende, High Street and le Dyte Ende were sold to other 'gentlemen of London'.

There would have been much dismay at the way these properties were being bought up by 'gentlemen of London'. Such speculators had no interest in local issues, unlike the The Holy Trinity Guild in particular which had played a leading role in the social as well as the religious life of the community. Its members now found themselves without the status or corporate income which had been the source of their power. It is interesting to see them a few years later acting together as 'feoffees' (town trustees) to buy back former guild or chantry land for the benefit of the community. In 1562 John Orpewode (probably the same John Oppwood who had looked after the Trinity Guild's plate before its confiscation), William Avery, Richard Hunt and Henry Butler bought back the

The old grammar school building. The school was founded by the Holy Trinity Guild but survived the guild's dissolution in 1549 because of a petition from the townspeople. This print also shows the original tower of the church before it was rebuilt in 1823. (Chipping Norton Museum)

Guildhall and other houses and lands from Anthony Ashfield of Barford with the express intention of holding them in trust for the town so that any profits could be used for such good purposes as the trustees and 'the most part of the substantial and honest men of Chipping Norton' should think meet. Early in the next century their successors presented the Guildhall to the new Corporation and it became the 'town hall' for more than two hundred years. Similarly, in 1572, in order to enhance the grammar school which the guild had originally founded, William Hunt and others on behalf of the inhabitants of the town purchased from William Avenell a house and garden on the south side of Church Street, and this may have been the site of the grammar school itself. A further enhancement took place in March 1590 when William Hutchins and nineteen other inhabitants bought from him another house and garden formerly the property of the chantry of St John, which he had himself purchased from Anthony Ashfield. The express purpose of this purchase was that the income from letting the property

> should forever be employed towards the maintenance of a schoolmaster, or as much thereof as should be thought necessary by consent of the said feoffees, to teach and instruct the children and scholars of all the inhab-

itants of the town of Chipping Norton, freely without paying anything therefore, in the Latin tongue.

Although the Chantry Commissioners had awarded an annual salary for the schoolmaster of £6 from the state, this allowed nothing for the maintenance of the buildings or other costs of running the school. Such costs would previously have been met out of the income of the guild and perhaps this was a consideration of the feoffees when buying back former chantry property.

The keeping of registers of baptisms, marriages and burials in every parish was one of the less controversial reforms brought in by Henry VIII. The first entries in the registers of Chipping Norton were made in 1550 but many of the earliest ones are now illegible. The first legible entry records the baptism of William the son of John Morgeayn in 1553; the earliest marriage record is that of John Gattewaye and Alys Moreland in 1560 and the first burial is that of Harry Boulton in 1564. A few years later the burial register illustrates the tragedy of families hit by an outbreak of plague in 1575: in little more than a week during September John Tynson, his wife Ales and three of their daughters died, and in October Richard Edkynes lost his wife and three sons in quick succession. Such outbreaks of plague were not uncommon and this one was not confined to Chipping Norton, the queen cancelling a proposed visit to Oxford because of it.

Chapter 6

Local and National Politics: the Charter and the Civil War

Chipping Norton prospered in the Elizabethan period. Whereas Burford and Witney had developed into cloth-making centres, Chipping Norton served as the largest market town for north-west Oxfordshire, where farmers and craftsmen from the surrounding area came to buy and sell. Shops opened around the market place, and trade was especially brisk on Wednesdays at the weekly market. In the middle of the market place, a simple market house was built by the townsmen in the sixteenth century to provide shelter for sellers and their customers. The annual fair in July brought more trade to the town, with separate areas for the sale of sheep, horses and cattle. Every transaction paid a toll and the lord of the manor's officials collected the money due to him.[1]

The Compton family held the manor of Chipping Norton but they never lived in the town, so their steward presided over the manorial court which enquired into local misdemeanours and punished offenders. The leading townsmen met in the Guildhall to make orders for the government of the town and to elect officials such as constables and aletasters, but their authority was limited. Nor were they able to acquire property for the benefit of the community, as the guild had done before its dissolution, and the use of individual townsmen to own communal property such as the guildhall as trustees for the town was not ideal. But what alarmed the town most of all was the arrival of a new lord of the manor.

---

1 The first part of this chapter incorporates a major contribution by Dr Adrienne Rosen based on her research into the events surrounding the grant of Chipping Norton's charter.

The Chadwell family had originally been yeoman farmers nearby at Great Rissington, with ambitions to rise in society. Michael Chadwell had lived in Chipping Norton for many years, and when in 1596 the Comptons decided to sell the manor it was Michael Chadwell who bought it. He was already unpopular and a few years earlier townspeople had pulled down walls around his land at night and attacked his servants. In 1603 there was a more serious incident at Primsdown when an angry crowd of townsmen, led by Henry Cornish and William Hunt, destroyed hedges, fences and gates on Chadwell's land and trampled his crops, claiming that he intended to plough up their common. Michael Chadwell's son Edward, who was disliked even more than his father, appointed Walter Thomas as steward of the manor, but then dismissed him and gave the position instead to Edmund Fryers of Kencot. The Chadwells applied to the king in 1606 and were granted two additional fairs at Chipping Norton each year to bring them extra revenue. After many years of government by distant lords of the manor who had largely left the townsmen to make their own decisions, they now had lords who were not only resident in the manor house in New Street but intent on exploiting their rights and increasing their income. Michael Chadwell was by now an elderly man and Edward was eagerly awaiting the day when he would inherit the manor. The prospects for good relations between the townsmen and their lord looked bleak.

Faced with this situation a small group of townsman met privately and decided on a strategy which had been successfully adopted by over a hundred other towns in the previous half century, including several local ones like Oxford, Banbury, Stow on the Wold, Chipping Campden and Evesham. Having agreed to share the considerable costs involved and to solicit support from various local gentlemen, they submitted a petition to the king on behalf of the town for a charter giving Chipping Norton the status of a borough governed by its own corporation which would be independent of the lord of the manor. The petition was successful and a royal charter of incorporation was duly granted by James I on 27th February 1607.[2]

---

2 Confusion is sometimes caused because the town seal bears the date 1606. This is because under the 'Old Style' calendar used at that time the new year began on 25 March and the charter was granted in February, which was reckoned as the eleventh month of the old year. When England adopted the more accurate Gregorian calendar in 1752, which has been used ever since, New Years Day reverted to 1 January and February became the second month of the new year. Therefore by modern reckoning the date is correctly given as 1607. The Charter itself uses the 'regnal year' – 'the fourth year of the reign of our sovereign lord king James'.

The royal charter granted by James I. It incorporated Chipping Norton as a borough governed by the Corporation of Bailiffs and Burgesses. (Chipping Norton Town Council)

The preamble, translated from the original Latin, stated:

Whereas our Borough of Chipping Norton... is an ancient Borough and Town and very Populous and the Inhabitants... have had and enjoyed divers Libertys Franchises freedoms and Preheminences... And whereas our well beloved subjects the inhabitants of the same Borough or Town have been most humble Petitioners that we would... reform and make new by our Letters Patent for the Aforesaid Inhabitants one Corporeal and compleat Body by the name of the Bailiffs and Burgesses of the Borough or Town of Chipping Norton.

The town was to be for ever hereafter a free borough, under a corporation composed of two Bailiffs and twelve Burgesses of the borough. The corporation was to possess a common seal, and to have power to purchase lands, to sue and be sued, to enact by-laws and to impose penalties for their non-observance. A drawing of the common seal was made in 1634 and it shows that the corporation chose the castle to symbolise the town's history, even though nothing remained of the building by that time.

The Bailiffs held office for a year only and were to be chosen out of the corporation on the Monday after Michaelmas Day. The custom was that they each nominated two Burgesses as their successors and the corporation then made their choice from among these four. They were obliged to take a special

Right: The charter authorised the use of a seal. This was recorded in the 1630s and is probably the original version. (Chipping Norton Town Council)

Below: The town seal used today. (Chipping Norton Town Council)

oath 'to do equal right between poor and rich after their cunning, wit and power, and after the Laws and Customs of the Realm and the Statutes for that purpose made; not to be of counsel in any quarrel, and to take nothing for their office of Justice of the Peace'. The two ex-Bailiffs served as Chamberlains to keep the borough accounts. The Burgesses were to continue in office for life, unless it became necessary to remove them, and appointments to vacancies were to be made by the surviving members of the Council. Two Sergeants-at-Mace were appointed to serve for proclamation of arrests, execution of processes and mandates, and other similar business; they were to carry maces of gold and silver engraved with the royal arms.

The charter gave the new corporation its own Court of Record, to be held every Monday, with all fines paid to the borough.[3] The weekly market on Wednesdays was also granted to the corporation, together with the traditional fair around the Feast of the Translation of St Thomas a Becket (7th July), and two new fairs around St Bartholomew's Day (24th August) and the Feast of

---

3 This court was only officially abolished in the 1960s, but had ceased to function before that.

SS Simon and Jude (28th October). The Bailiffs and Burgesses were also to appoint and maintain the schoolmaster of the grammar school.

William Hunt and William Diston were named as the first Bailiffs, and the first Burgesses were to be Henry Cornish, Thomas Hyatt, Thomas Fawler, John Willetts, Mark Preston, Richard Berry, Henry Carrick, Thomas Cornish, Christopher Needle, Edward Averill and John Sidbury (or Sudbury) and Walter Thomas. These were the townsmen who had petitioned for the charter. Walter Thomas, who had been dismissed by Edward Chadwell as steward of the manor, was now to become the first Town Clerk, and he must have had some legal training. The others were from a variety of trades: William Hunt, Henry Cornish and Mark Preston were mercers, Thomas Fawler and John Willetts were drapers, Richard Berry was both mercer and linen draper and Thomas Hyatt was a maltster who owned the Swan in West Street, while Christopher Needle was a glover and Edward Averill was a shoemaker. As in most market towns of the period, the leading tradesmen were retailers selling a variety of goods to customers from a wide area, while others were involved in the production of food, drink and clothing.

The townsmen's victory over the Chadwells appeared to be complete. With the grant of the charter, all the tolls paid at the weekly market and the three annual fairs would henceforth go to the borough instead of the lord of the manor, and the new Court of Record would also divert business and income from the manorial courts to the borough. Michael Chadwell and his son Edward were outraged and they resolved to overthrow the charter. This was not an idle threat, for in 1606–07 the townsmen of Stow were engaged in a struggle to defend their charter against the new lord of the manor and eventually lost their new-found rights and liberties.

On Monday 13th April 1607, soon after the charter had come into force, the Bailiffs and Burgesses assembled in the upper room of the Guildhall. Their borough court session was under way at the upper end of the hall when Edmund Fryers, the Chadwells' steward, climbed the stairs and burst into the room at the head of a boisterous crowd to disrupt the proceedings. The Bailiffs persuaded them to depart but half an hour later Fryers returned with even more supporters 'in disordered and riotous manner', sat down on one of the benches and refused to leave. The Bailiffs protested that they were sitting as Justices of the Peace in the king's service, to which Fryers responded, 'I care not for that, I am as good a Justice of the Peace as any of you all, I will stay here in despite of you'. After a heated argument he was bound over to appear at the next Assizes in Oxford and one of the sergeants took him away, although his supporters boasted in the alehouses that they had overturned the charter.

The fair on 7th July brought further strife and disorder, as rival officials for the new corporation and for Michael Chadwell attempted to collect tolls on purchases and fees for setting up stalls. With the streets crowded with livestock and farmers, the Bailiffs attempted to read a proclamation at the high cross in the market place directing that the horse market should be moved from its usual site in Horsefair to New Street, while the cattle market should move from New Street to West Street. Chadwell's bailiff countered with a proclamation ordering that the markets should stay in their accustomed places, causing great confusion.

Having failed to threaten the townsmen into submission, in October 1607 the Chadwells turned to the law and brought a suit in the Court of Star Chamber alleging that the townsmen had conspired against their rights as lords of the manor. The Bailiffs and Burgesses had all contributed to a fund for the defence of their charter and they responded with a suit against the Chadwells. Both sides made exaggerated claims of assault and disorder, and many witnesses for both parties were summoned to give their version of events. In 1609 the judges decided in favour of the townsmen and ordered Michael and Edward Chadwell to pay large fines and be imprisoned in the Fleet Prison in London, while Michael Chadwell was also ordered to make a humiliating acknowledgement of his offences at the next fair in Chipping Norton; however, on his petition that he was now very old he was excused imprisonment, and the fines were never paid.

The Chadwells had already decided that the manor of Chipping Norton was not the investment they had hoped for. Edward Chadwell was deeply indebted and he and his father were pursued by creditors. In November 1608 the Chadwells sold the title, rights and a small part of the land of the manor of Chipping Norton to John Throckmorton, gentleman of Little Rollright for £600. They retained the manor house in New Street and a substantial amount of land, but they were no longer lords of the manor and in time their house became known instead as a 'mansion house'. Michael Chadwell died in 1610. The title of Lord of the Manor of Chipping Norton was held for the next sixty years by the owners of the Little Rollright estate. John Throckmorton sold it in 1612 to William Blower, a wealthy Londoner, who died in 1618 leaving his estate to his sister Mary and her husband Henry Dixon. The Dixons had lands in Kent but their eldest son Edward lived at Little Rollright from 1634 until 1654, and on his death in 1660 the manor of Chipping Norton descended to his son Henry who sold it to Thomas Chamberlayne of Oddington in 1663.

With the defeat of the Chadwells the newly-created corporation was safe,

One of the corporation's 17th-century silver gilt maces. They were symbols of the corporation's authority derived from its royal charter. There were originally two carried by the Sergeants at Mace on ceremonial occasions. (Chipping Norton Town Council)

and in 1628 it passed a set of by-laws. Burgesses were required to behave 'orderly, discreetly and soberly' at meetings, and to keep their proceedings confidential. The Bailiffs were responsible for providing twenty leather buckets, ladders and hooks at the guildhall, to pull down thatch in case of a fire in the town. Anyone who was elected a Burgess and refused to serve was to be fined £4. Another by-law forbade any person to house strangers within the borough without the consent of the corporation, under a penalty of ten shillings a month. No one was to exercise any trade in the town unless he had been made a freeman of the borough by birth, apprenticeship or purchase; the penalty for breaking this law was 13s 4d a month. This and similar restrictions remained in force up to the time when the new corporation came into being under the Municipal Corporations Act of 1835.

The Burgesses were to meet at the Guildhall every Sunday morning and evening 'before the little bell there called the Saints' Bell shall have done ringing', together with the 'Town Clerk and Attorneys of the Borough Court, and the officers in their decent robes of office, and accompany the Bailiffs to the Parish Church, and return with them to the Guildhall after the Sermon, and there reverently take their leaves of them.' For bearing the maces as they walked before the corporation on these occasions the Sergeants received one shilling a week.

The rivalry that had flared between the lord of the manor and the new corporation of Bailiffs and Burgesses when the charter granted them rights previously enjoyed by the lord, does not seem to have recurred after the Chadwells sold the title. In 1668 the Bailiffs and Burgesses finally acquired the lordship of the manor for themselves by purchasing it from Thomas Chamberlayne of Oddington, who had himself bought it only five years previously. One important change, however, was that the value of the manor had been greatly reduced by this time because when the Chadwells sold the title to John Throckmorton in 1608 they had retained most of its land for themselves. This possibly amounted to as much as 600 acres of arable in the open fields, 68 acres of meadow and pasture and 26 acres of woodland, plus the site of the former castle, their own manor house in New Street, a watermill and various properties leased to tenants. All this the Chadwells kept, and it was only the title with the manorial rights and some small remnants of land which they sold, and which were eventually purchased by the Bailiffs and Burgesses. Even this was not without controversy because it soon leaked out that in order to raise the sum needed to make the purchase the corporation had misused £196 13s 4d of charitable bequests entrusted to their care. As a consequence an inquiry held in Oxford in 1686 ordered the Bailiffs and Burgesses, and their successors, to repay £25 a year out of manorial income to the town's charities.[4]

William Averill, a Bailiff in the Corporation and son of one of the original Burgesses named in the charter, was one of several leading citizens with Puritan sympathies in the period leading up to the Civil War. Like the Pilgrim Fathers before him, he chose to emigrate rather than suffer the frustration of seeing the Church of England under Charles I and Archbishop Laud adopt high church practices which to Puritans seemed only a step away from Catholicism. According to a plaque erected in the parish church in 1928 by his American descendants, he had sailed to America in 1635, settling at Ipswich Colony in Massachusetts Bay.

For others who stayed there were terrible times ahead. Religious and constitutional differences between king and parliament divided the nation. Already in 1638 the king's attempt to collect Ship Money from inland counties had been met with strong objections in Oxfordshire, and it was reported that the inhabitants of Chipping Norton 'began to dispute the extent of their liberties', which may have been a genuine dispute over the right of Chipping Norton to collect the tax from people in Over Norton or it may have been a delaying tactic because of general reluctance to pay as was evident in other parts of the county. Disputes such as this over the rights of king and parliament and religious differences between Puritans and high church Anglicans led to Civil War. The first battle was fought in 1642 at Edgehill less than 20 miles from Chipping Norton, and for the next four years the town shared with the rest of the region the horrors and hardships of a very bitter war. The king made his headquarters at Oxford and the whole county was ravaged for money, supplies and men to support his army and court. Chipping Norton had the disadvantage of being close to the county boundary and the shifting frontier between the two sides, so that it would have been pressured by

---

4 This amount was still paid annually by their successors the Borough Council until 1974.

demands and threats from both Royalist and Parliamentarian local commanders. One of the worst was the Roundhead Colonel Purefoy at nearby Compton Wynyates whose men terrorised a large area of south Warwickshire and north Oxfordshire. Even closer was Colonel Gerard Croker at Hook Norton, notorious for his harshness in collecting supplies for the Royalists. Horses, wagons, livestock of all kinds, crops, timber, leather and metal goods were requisitioned, with inevitable loss and sometimes ruin to local people. There were constant demands for money. In 1643 the king imposed a levy on the county of over £61,000, (far more than the Ship Money tax) of which much of Chadlington Hundred's share amounting to £147 per week was probably extracted from Chipping Norton.

Armies moving through the region were forced to spread their march over a wide area so that they could live off the resources of towns and villages in the countryside. The ordinary soldiers slept rough, under hedges or in barns and outbuildings and the lucky ones together with officers were billeted in the houses of local people along the route, with little consideration for the householders, especially if they showed reluctance to take them or were suspected of supporting the other side. Crops were trampled and livestock killed or driven off to feed the soldiers, and houses were plundered for money and other goods. Chipping Norton was on a major route and would have suffered often in this way. In 1645 a party of Cavaliers after spending a night in Chipping Norton are said to have plundered every house in the town of 'whatsoever was of value' When William Coleman died in the town in 1646 an inventory of his goods which should have included his clothes recorded that he had only a coat, hat and a pair of boots 'his wearing garments being plundered by soldiers'. The previous year Chipping Norton was allegedly the scene of one of the worst atrocities reported in Oxfordshire, according to a Royalist news-sheet. When Parliament's army under the Earl of Essex advanced across the north of the county on its way to relieve the siege of Gloucester it camped for one night in and around Chipping Norton. The men were in a desperate state after several days and nights of marching and sleeping rough, with very little to eat because the area had already been stripped bare by the Royalists. In the morning as tired and hungry Roundhead soldiers filled the market place, a woman in the watching crowd dared to shout out 'God bless the Cavaliers'. She was seized by some of the soldiers, stripped and beaten and then tied to the back of a cart and dragged along the road behind it, being repeatedly whipped and beaten as it set off down New Street and up the Worcester road. She was left for dead about two miles out of the town. Apart from particular events like these there was the continual anxiety and privation felt by people trying to cope in the danger and uncertainty of wartime, particularly women trying to care for their families on their own. Disease was another consequence of war. Burial registers do not survive for Chipping Norton during the disruption of wartime, but elsewhere in the county death rates among civilians soared as a result of plague and fever often spread by undernourished soldiers and easily caught by the population of towns and villages where they lodged. Richard Shelfoxe of Over Norton was struck down without time to make a will in 1645 and the witnesses to his last wishes testified to 'the disease called the plague or pestilence being much in Over Norton'.

The inhabitants of Chipping Norton were divided in their loyalties. The evidence of William Avery, Henry Cornish, William Diston and others suggest that there was a strong Puritan element in the Corporation which would incline them towards Parliament. The Town Clerk, however, was a Royalist. Michael Chadwell, grandson of the former lord of the manor who had opposed the charter, fought for the king and perhaps among other considerations saw the war as a way to settle old scores. After the war both he and his brother-in-law Robert Wharton had their lands sequestered by Parliament as a punishment and Chadwell was probably forced to sell or mortgage most of his former manorial property before he died in 1656. Meanwhile William Diston petitioned the Council of State for compensation for the losses he had suffered through supporting Parliament, claiming that both he and his elderly uncle Henry Cornish had suffered imprisonment and had only been released on payment of a large sum of money, including £600 on behalf of Cornish. As a result the Treasury Commissioners were instructed to pay him £200.

Even the vicar of Chipping Norton, John Norgrove, was a moderate Puritan and apparently well liked by his parishioners, helping many of them make their wills. Appointed in 1626 he continued to hold the living throughout the war and survived the first ejections of Anglican clergy by the Puritans in 1648–49. A more radical purge finally removed him in 1654 and he died in February 1659. He was succeeded by Robert Eaton for a short period and then in March 1656 by the Puritan minister Stephen Ford. Ford seems to have been sufficiently well thought of by the Council of State for them to recommend an increase in the value of the living from £56 a year to £100 but he was not so popular with the surviving high church element in Chipping Norton, and on one occasion was violently attacked in his pulpit by Anne Clemens, a baker's wife. She 'tore his cloak, and with some others assisting her, forced him down from the pulpit and set up an Episcopal one in his room.' When the monarchy was restored in 1660 and with it the Anglican church, Ford resigned the living without waiting to be ejected and held nonconformist meetings in a private house in the town where his followers formed an Independent (later Presbyterian) congregation. He continued to suffer for his nonconformity and when threats were made against his life eventually took refuge in London, becoming pastor of a congregation in Miles Lane, Cannon Street where he continued to preach during the plague, when others fled into the country.

For the next twenty years the church was without a legal incumbent until the appointment of the Rev Edward Redrobe in September 1683. For part of this long vacancy it was served by a Puritan curate, Edmund Hall, MA, Fellow of Pembroke College, Oxford, who epitomised the uncertainty that some men felt in choosing sides during the religious and political strife of the seventeenth century. During the Civil War he had fought for Parliament, but seems still to have believed in the principle of monarchy and wrote against what he saw as Cromwell's pretensions with great bitterness. For this he was committed to prison for twelve months, still attacking the government in published pamphlets. In Chipping Norton he is said to have 'obtained the character from some of a fantastical, and from others of an edifying preacher'. However, at the Restoration he was prepared to conform to the Church of England and in 1680 became rector of Great Rissington, where he died in 1687.

Joseph Davis 'a zealous and pious preacher' fared less well. His father John Davis had been a Burgess of the Corporation but lost his position and wealth at the Restoration. Joseph was apprenticed to a mercer in Coventry where he described himself as a Seventh Day Baptist. Later he returned to Chipping Norton and soon after the Restoration was twice arrested by troops who rifled his house and took away his goods. Altogether he was kept a prisoner for ten years in Oxford Castle, and finally after his wife's death from consumption was released by the king. He set up as a linen draper in London, and it was he who offered refuge to Stephen Ford. He died in 1707.

There were also Quakers in the town and among those who suffered for their beliefs were members of the Tidmarsh family. In 1660 Giles Tidmarsh was sent to jail for not paying towards the upkeep of the 'steeple house' (i.e. the parish church), but appears to have been released in October 1661 as part of a gesture of clemency by Charles II towards nonconformists. The following year, however, his name, together with that of Thomas Tidmarsh, appeared on a list of people who were fined. He had been summoned to appear before the Archdeacon to answer for his unorthodox Quaker wedding and was further charged with disrespectful behaviour – presumably refusing to doff his hat to the Archdeacon. Later he received another term of imprisonment, from which he was finally released with a number of others as a result of the Declaration of Indulgence issued by Charles II in 1672. William Tidmarsh of Sarsden who was fined for attending a meeting at Stow on the Wold in 1681 may have belonged to the same family.

In this period after the Restoration when nonconformists were constantly harassed and punished, there were a number of men in the town eager to inform against them such as Thomas Samuel, Thomas Pannier, Thomas Houlton, Richard Adcock and others. Robert Werg, while constable, was active in 'informing against dissenters, watching to discover their meetings and making distress on their goods'. Thomas Lodge also 'set himself violently to persecute the Dissenters and resolved to suppress them entirely' according to sources which recorded the sufferings of nonconformists at this time but also took delight in recording what was clearly seen as divine judgement on their persecutors, who in these colourful accounts invariably fell ill or lost their worldly goods and died in miserable poverty. The passing of the Toleration Act in 1689 put an end to the persecutions and thenceforth there was religious if not political liberty for all Protestant nonconformists, and the year 1694 saw the building of a Presbyterian chapel in New Street.

Chapter 7

Life in Seventeenth-Century Chipping Norton

Henry Cornish, who had played a part in obtaining the town's royal charter and served for many years as a member of the new Corporation of Bailiffs and Burgesses, had been born in 1576 and prospered as a mercer (a dealer in cloth and other goods). He married as his first wife Elizabeth the daughter of Alderman Thomas Browne of Woodstock and became a leading figure in the commercial and civic life of Chipping Norton. He came to own a considerable amount of property including the White Hart Inn (though he did not live there or run it). His sister Jane married William Diston and the Cornishes and Distons were among the leading families in the town at this time. In later life they suffered at the hands of the Royalists for their Puritan beliefs during the Civil War, but it may have been Puritan principles, which laid great emphasis on charity towards the poor, that inspired Henry Cornish to make bequests for which he is still remembered today. The most important of these was the row of eight almshouses in Church Street, founded in 1640 and bequeathed to the town by his will dated 1650.[1] His gift is commemorated by an inscription and the old stone gateway has 'Remember the Poor' above it. He stipulated that the inmates were to be eight poor widows who had lived in the town for seven years and were 'of honest and Godly life and conversation'. He also left twenty shillings a year for the maintenance of the property, and two shillings per week to provide bread for the inmates 'to each of them three pennyworth on every Monday'. These almshouses and their inmates attracted further bequests over subsequent years from other benefactors. In addition, Cornish left to his nephew Thomas Diston twelve other cottages situated in Chipping Norton which together with others had been purchased

---

1 Modernised in the 1950s and converted to four rather larger dwellings.

The Henry Cornish Almshouses. Founded in 1640 they were intended for eight poor widows 'of honest and godly life and conversation'.

from Sir William Cope of Hanwell (another leading Puritan).[2] It was stipulated that the rents of these were not to be increased 'but remain for ever to be let at the rents they are now for the benefit of poor people' and the tenants should be honest, peaceful and religious persons who had lived in the town for seven years. He left money to provide annually coats for two poor men and gowns for two poor women and 4*d* each (a 'groat') to no less than 40 widows. At the other end of the social scale he left money to the corporation of Bailiffs and Burgesses, of which he had been a member from the beginning, to establish an annual dinner at the White Hart. This became known as the Bailiffs' Feast and continued to be held for nearly two hundred years after his death.

In spite of his wealth and standing in the community, there was a less happy side to Henry Cornish's life. Of the twelve children born to his wife Elizabeth, ten died in childhood and the remaining two in their thirties. After Elizabeth's own death he married again but the relationship may have been

---

2 One of these cottages was on the site of the present 72 West Street and is referred to in its deeds. The others have not been identified.

a strained one. He wrote his last will secretly with the help of friends and cancelled any previous wills which he claimed he had been forced to make under pressure from Sarah his second wife and her family, whom he accused of taking advantage of his old age and illness. He left her money and a home during her lifetime but after that everything reverted to his own Cornish relations and to the Diston family. His final request, a very typical Puritan sentiment, was that his funeral sermon should be preached by 'some able, godly orthodox divine' and that he should be buried in the middle aisle of the parish church, close to his son and daughter.

Under the terms of the charter in 1607 the Bailiffs and Burgesses had been given the right to appoint 'one fit honest and learned man to the office of a Schoolmaster' to run the grammar school. This occupied a building in Church Street on the site of the present vicarage and an old print shows a substantial stone building with mullioned windows which might date from this period. Few details other than the names of some of the masters have survived. From time to time bequests were made, usually to augment the salary of the master. Robert Hutchins gave £60 partly for this purpose and in 1672 Frances Barnes left the considerable sum of £300. Although sometimes referred to as a 'free' grammar school, it appears only to have been free to the two boys nominated for free places by the corporation. Other pupils paid termly fees which also helped to supplement the master's salary.

In 1697 the choir of singers in the church were given permission by the vicar and churchwardens to build a gallery 'all the breadth of the middle aisle of the church, rising from the ground in tiers till they reached the top of the rails of the belfrey ... none to come and set there but what the singers thought fit, and such only as learned the singing.' This gallery remained until removed in the nineteenth century. Who the 'singers' were is not known but several seventeenth century inventories include musical instruments such as 'a pair of virginals' and a 'base viol' among personal possessions, suggesting that music making was a part of people's lives. The viol belonged to John Littleford who died in May 1624. He had very few belongings when he died and his bass viol in its case, worth 10s, was the most valuable thing he owned.

Wills and inventories of people living in the town at this time afford a fascinating insight into the personal details of their lives.[3] Thomas Henslo lived in

---

3 About 600 probate documents from the period 1545 to 1730 survive from Chipping Norton and Over Norton in the Oxfordshire Record Office. All have now been transcribed, plus some from the Public Record Office, thanks to the dedicated work of the Chipping Norton Historical Research Group. Copies of the transcripts are being

a very modest three-roomed house in 1613 consisting of a hall (the living room), a chamber where he slept and a kitchen, but he had horses, cattle, a pig and a flock of 62 sheep together worth £25 and crops worth £38. Though not poor, he was still living in a small old-fashioned style of house, but for those who could afford it the early seventeenth century saw a widespread rebuilding and improvement of their homes. Bedrooms or 'chambers' on an upper floor reached by a staircase became more common, in place of mere storage lofts with a ladder in an otherwise one-storey house. Alice Deacon's inventory in 1600 mentions a 'window cloth' – oiled cloth stretched across the opening to keep out rain but admit some rather dim light, but better-off people were now able to afford glass. This and the fashionable 'wainscot' panelling used to cover the walls and make the rooms more comfortable were still so valuable that they were sometimes separately bequeathed in wills like that of Joan Carrick who left to her son Thomas 'all the seiling and wainscot in the hall and the screen in the nether chamber'. Joan and Henry Carrick were clearly prosperous, Henry describing himself as 'yeoman' in his will. Their house was also a tavern and there were a number of hostelries of various sorts in Chipping Norton, serving the needs of travellers, visitors to the markets and fairs, as well as locals. The White Hart, probably already old by the seventeenth century, always seems to have been the most important inn and is well documented with detailed inventories of the rooms and their furnishings (including 12 pewter chamber pots and several four-post beds in 1633[4]). Some of the rooms have interesting names like the Hereford Chamber, the Queen's Arms Chamber and the Gatehouse Chamber. Down in the cellar were 7½ hogsheads of beer, French wine, sack, brandy and sherry. Henry Cornish bought the White Hart at some time and bequeathed it to his nephew William Diston, who ran it and issued tokens from that address. In 1670 Thomas Frayne was another innholder, probably also in the High Street where he held a lease of 'sheep ground' in front of a property to the north of the Katherine Wheel (the Crown and Cushion today). There is also a house in New Street, just below Distons Lane, with 'Thomas Frayne 1635' on the front, but this is probably too early to be the innkeeper, perhaps his father. Thomas Frayne's inn in 1670 was not very big with a hall, parlour, kitchen and buttery and four

---

deposited in the Record Office and it is hoped that a fuller account of the work will be published at a future date. The material in this chapter draws on only a small fraction of the documents.

4 One of these magnificently carved four post beds remained in the White Hart until it ceased to be an inn in 2004.

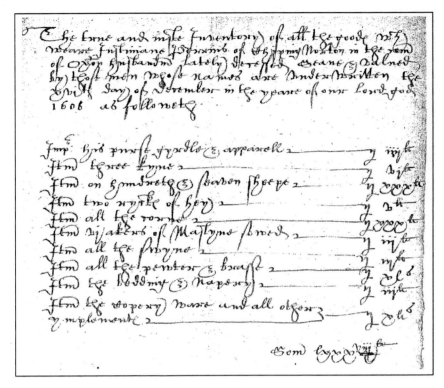

Part of the inventory of Justinian Perrin, 1606. He was a small farmer and his property included 107 sheep, two ricks of hay, corn, six acres of maslin (a mixed crop of wheat and rye) and some pigs. These and the rest of his household goods and belongings were valued at £88. He had debts owing to him of a further £8 12s 6d. The valuation was done by four local men but only one of them, Richard Heydon, could write his name, and he presumably wrote this very neat document.

upstairs 'chambers', two over the hall and parlour and two described as 'little' over the buttery and the entry, though one of these was large enough to contain three beds. The furnishing suggests a busy household: the best bedroom had a four-poster and a truckle bed for a servant or child and there were 18 pairs of sheets, 10 tablecloths, 4 spits and six dozen pewter dishes. There is mention of curtains and curtain rods in the windows and a picture hanging in the parlour – quite comfortable furnishings for the seventeenth century.

Four-post beds with a tester and curtains provided shelter from draughts and a degree of privacy when landings were not common and people walked through one bedroom to reach the others. When Thomas Turner died in 1632 he divided his house equally between his widow, who could go on occupying the hall, chamber over the hall, chamber over the entry and half the backside (probably a lean-to behind the house), while his son got the shop (he was a tailor), the chamber over the shop, the buttery and the other half of the back-side. Thomas added a note in his will saying 'if my sonne Christopher doe find that hir going up and down to be a trouble throw (through) the chamber over the shop I doe enjoine him to make hir a stayer in the hawle'. This situation of widows and grown up children sharing the same house could be a problem, and when John Lancaster died in 1604 his will stipulated that his daughter and son-in-law could live in the house with his widow 'if they doe behave themselves dutifully to their mother, els not'! Another concern for some when they were writing their last wills was to specify where they should be buried. For ordinary folk it was enough to be buried in the churchyard, but some were more specific, like Henry Carrick in 1599 who asked that he should be buried 'by the ewe tree on the left hande neareunto myne ancestors'. Only the most important people in the community could claim the right to burial within the church itself, and fittingly Henry Cornish was one who did.

Wills and inventories also illustrate the variety of trades and occupations in the town. William Littleford was a miller in 1621 and occupied 'the mill-house', a watermill belonging to the lord of the manor. The expensive luxury of glass windows at this time should have made the trade of glazier a pros-perous one but William Knowles a glazier who died in 1634 prefaced his will with the words 'As for my worldly goods which is not much ...' and left every-thing to his wife except for some pieces of timber which were all his daughter and her husband inherited from him. A complete contrast in the same year was the will of Thomas Letch, a tanner. Tanners were among the wealthiest tradesmen in Chipping Norton at this time, probably making use of plentiful skins and hides from the animals kept in the surrounding countryside and bought and sold in the markets and fairs. Leather was a widely used commodity[5] and such was the importance of the trade that the Corporation appointed two Leather Sealers annually to check on the quality of leather being sold. The tanning process involved using large quantities of oak bark (because of the tannic acid it contained) and other less wholesome things like bird and dog faeces to soften the hides while soaking for long periods in pits. Letch leased a house in New Street plus other property and might have owned the same tannery that survived in Distons Lane until the twentieth century. His goods and chattels were worth £602, a considerable sum at that time, most of which was the value of his stock of 470 hides at different stages of the tanning process, 360 calfskins and 55 loads of bark. This was industry on a

---

5 Before the Industrial Revolution the leather industry is considered by some author-ities to have been second only to the wool cloth trade in economic importance.

considerable scale, supplying leather to craftsmen in the area who produced boots, shoes, belts, saddles, harness, straps and other heavy leather goods, or to curriers who further dressed it to the softer quality required for glove making and lighter goods.

Tanning had to be done in a particular place where the pits had been constructed, but the various stages of cloth manufacture were carried out in the homes of spinners and weavers and other tradesmen as a domestic operation. John Tuston of Over Norton worked in the cloth finishing trade as a shearman. This was part of the fulling process which involved taking rolls of cloth from the weavers, soaking and scouring them with fuller's earth and then improving the texture by raising the nap and then clipping the surface with huge shears. When he died in 1605 the inventory of his goods included two pairs of shears valued at 10s and 3s 4d and some teasels worth 8d. The teasels were set in a wooden frame and used to raise the nap of the cloth. He also owned a little horse, an old saddle and bridle and a 'wanty' – a strap used for securing a load such as rolls of cloth onto the horse's back. So we have a complete picture of him going about his daily work. Similarly we get a picture of the work of John Symones who lived in Over Norton lodge and had the rather unusual job of warrener, possibly keeping an eye on that same rabbit warren that had upset the people of Over Norton over a century before. His possessions included two 'hay nets', three ferrets and a gun.

Many of these tradesmen supplemented their living by doing a little farming, but William Smyth, who died a few days before Christmas in 1628, was a 'husbandman' – a full-time farmer. His house consisted of a hall, parlour and buttery with two upstairs chambers and was quite comfortably furnished. His total belongings were valued at £138 16s 8d, most of which was the value of his crops and livestock worth £105 19s. From his probate inventory we get a good idea of farming practice in seventeenth-century Chipping Norton. He grew wheat, barley and pulses (probably beans), on his strips in the open fields. When he died in December there were six acres of winter wheat standing in the field and more from the previous crop in his barn, some threshed and some waiting to be threshed as needed. There was also barley in a hovel and some already malted for brewing. A rick of beans and hay stood in the yard as winter fodder for the livestock, which consisted of fifty sheep, five horses, six 'beasts' and two weaning calves, four hogs and six store pigs. The horses, worth £18 with their harness, provided the power on the farm and pulled his plough, two harrows, a long cart and a dung cart. Interestingly, he also had a tanhouse with vats in it, suggesting that he was tanning hides from his own livestock at home rather than buying leather from John Letch.

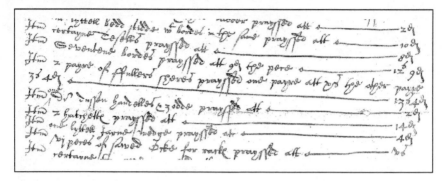

Extract from the inventory of John Tuston of Over Norton, a shearman involved in the cloth finishing trade. His equipment listed here includes boards on which to lay the cloth, teasels for raising the nap and two pairs of shears for cropping its surface. He died in 1601.

Very occasionally an inventory lists items other than general household goods and furniture, giving an insight into the minds of seventeenth-century people. William Turner, another quite wealthy tanner, died in 1617 and among his possessions were three books – a collection of Froissart's historical *Chronicles*, a bible and a book with the unusual title of *The Heavenly Sale of Salt*. This Puritan propaganda work in the form of a dialogue had been published in London in 1611 and is another hint at the perhaps widespread support for Puritanism in Chipping Norton. Turner was one of the Corporation's Sergeants at Mace.

People could buy locally made products direct from a craftsman at his workshop, and there would have been fewer retail shops around the market place at this period than there are today. There were some shops, however, importing fancy goods and items not produced in the town. Samuel Harris clearly ran one of these and had a stock of hats worth as much as £130. Poorer people in the villages, who could perhaps not afford his prices, decorated their rather cheaper hats with ribbons bought from a travelling chapman like another William Smith who died in 1628 and had in his house 'small wares' worth 5s.

Some shopkeepers in the second half of the seventeenth century issued their own form of coinage called tokens, equivalent to pennies, halfpennies or farthings. There was a general shortage of small change at the time because no copper coins were minted during the Commonwealth. Tokens bore the name of the issuing tradesman and were only redeemable at his shop, thus providing a form of advertising as well as local currency. Among Chipping Norton tradesmen and innkeepers who produced tokens were Michael Cornish a mercer, William Diston 'at the White Hart', Samuel Farmer, apothecary, Richard Groves, grocer and Mathias Troute a chandler. They were substantial property owners and probably among the leading tradesmen in the town. The issuing of tokens was eventually banned in 1672.

In the unsettled years immediately after the Civil War travellers were often confronted by highwaymen, some of whom were disillusioned Cavaliers unable or unwilling to return to normal civilian life after the excitements of war and the defeat of their cause. Notorious among them was the self-styled 'Captain' James Hind of Chipping Norton, born in 1616 the son of a respectable saddler, but who left the town and became involved with a gang of thieves in London. He is said to have joined the Royalist army when war broke out, no doubt tempted as many were by the prospect of adventure and the scope for legitimate robbery. After the defeat of the king he took to the road and became the subject of ballads and legends, earning a romantic popular image by his alleged wit and gallantry towards ladies, and his reputation for being generous to the poor. A typical story recounts that he was forced by his own needs to rob a poor farmer returning from Wantage market but kept his promise to repay him with interest a week later. As an ex-Cavalier he seems to have specialized in robbing Parliamentarians and is reputed to have attempted to hold up Cromwell's coach on one occasion. In spite of such stories he was undoubtedly a menace to travellers. Anthony Wood heard of his exploits and described him as 'a little dapper, desperate fellow'. Hind rejoined the army to fight for Charles II at the battle of Worcester in 1652 but was captured soon afterwards, and it was in that city that he was finally condemned to be hanged, drawn and quartered.

Chapter 8

Local Government under the Bailiffs and Burgesses

During the eighteenth century the town remained largely self-supporting, most of the needs of the inhabitants being supplied by local farmers and tradesmen. Their shops, workshops and inns were in the main streets of the town and behind many were the medieval burgage plots which provided space for stables and pigsties as well as orchards and gardens, for some tradesmen in this period were also involved in small-scale farming. A very noticeable change to the appearance of the market place happened during this century. The houses, inns and shops surrounding it would probably have been two- or three-storey gabled buildings, a few perhaps even of timber framed construction, but these styles were becoming outdated and from about the 1730s nearly all of them were replaced, or given a new façade in the classical style which was so fashionable in the Georgian period. The new fronts were taller, often with a parapet hiding the eaves, dormers in the roof and sash windows replacing the old casements. They were fronted with ashlar stone if the owners could afford it and, in the wealthiest examples, with rusticated stonework, projecting quoins and arched or 'Venetian' windows. Although individual houses vary, the overall style is mostly uniform and the collective effect must have been as fine as any street in the county outside Oxford. The transformation suggests that the eighteenth century was a prosperous time in Chipping Norton.

Further out, but still part of the urban structure, were several farmhouses in an older style, with stables, barns and outbuildings. Agriculture remained a significant occupation for many of the inhabitants, either as small farmers owning or renting 'yardlands' (a collection of scattered arable strips probably equal to just over 20 acres in Chipping Norton), or as skilled workers like shepherds and carters, or simply labourers. Every householder had the right to graze a few animals on the commons and for some this may have provided an important element in the survival of a family not far above subsistence level.

18th century buildings in Market Place. With their expensive dressed ashlar facing, Venetian or round windows, projecting 'rusticated' stonework at the corners and careful proportions, they are typical of the new styles which transformed the appearance of Chipping Norton. They also suggest a prosperous community at this time.

The last of the old style buildings. The old Red Lion Inn survived until 1893. It gives a clue to the appearance of the market place before the 18th century rebuilding. There are other examples of this style in New Street. (Chipping Norton Museum)

The huge open fields surrounded the town with their intricate pattern of furlongs divided into narrow ridge and furrow strips for arable cultivation.[1] There were also large areas of meadow and pasture like the 'Great Common below the Town' where cattle, horses and sheep grazed at set times of the year, or the rougher all-year grazing provided by Southcombe and the Heath.

The Bailiffs and Burgesses, now also lords of the manor, exercised their function of government not only as the Corporation, but also through the manorial Court Baron and Court Leet, but the distinction between these bodies and their once separate roles seems to have become blurred in practice by the eighteenth century. The Bailiffs were Justices of the Peace for the Borough and held Quarter Sessions but much of their jurisdiction seems to have been carried out through the manorial courts where all kinds of minor offences against the by-laws, such as obstructing the highway, pollution of watercourses, irregularities in repairing the highways, etc, referred to as 'nuisances', were tried and the culprits fined. They also enforced market regulations. Thomas Robinson was fined in 1764 for having bought some fowls nearly an hour before the bell rang for the opening of the market. This practice, officially called 'forestalling', seems to have become so frequent that in 1776 the Corporation, having received complaints 'that divers carriers, higglers and other persons had bought up geese, ducks, fowls, butter, cheese and other victuals before the same hath been brought into the Market Place for sale and before the Market Bell hath rung, to the great prejudice of the inhabitants of the Borough', issued an order at one of their Corporation meetings banning such activity. They resolved 'that Mr Town Clerk do cause the above order to be made public by having the same cried on a market day and sticking up papers in the Market Place'. Local residents, however, so long as they were not intending to resell, could buy before the ringing of the market bell at 12 noon.

From time to time people were fined for building on the waste land of the manor, but their fines might be more in the nature of a quit rent payable if the encroaching building was allowed to continue in existence. Others had caused obstructions by leaving timber or stones in the highway or by leaving wagons in the streets. In 1757 Thomas Crutch was presented by the jury as having caused a great nuisance by milking his cows in the public market place morning and evening, which was 'very offensive to the inhabitants'. Even more offensive must have been the dung heap left in Church Street by Ned

---

1 Only small fragments of this once widespread ridge and furrow now survive, near Oldner House and on the north side of Church Lane.

Tinson and presented on two occasions. In 1785 Mr George Matthews was charged with having his weights too light. In 1788 the guard of the mail coach was presented for wilfully and repeatedly throwing down the common wall. This suggests an early example of 'road rage' perhaps directed against alterations to the line of the main road resulting from enclosure.

The courts also dealt with matters relating to the commons and other lands of the manor. The jury drew up annually a list of regulations governing farming practice on the unenclosed land in the manor and specified the dates of opening and closing ('breaking and heyning') the commons. Animals were excluded from the commons for several months to allow the grass to grow, and then re-admitted. Roadside verges were similarly controlled. The day of 'breaking' the commons was greeted with relief and celebration by those with livestock and was almost a public holiday in the town. The types and numbers of animals that each occupier of a house or yardland was entitled to graze were set by the jury. It was particularly important that the commons should not be impoverished by overstocking, or that infectious beasts should not be allowed to mix with other people's animals. Animals grazed unlawfully or straying off the common were impounded and only restored to their owners on payment of a fine. These regulations were policed by the Drivers, and offenders were brought before the court, the steward imposing fines paid partly to the Drivers as a reward for their vigilance and partly to the lord of the manor. The wastes were also important as a source of fuel and for collecting animal dung for fertilising gardens and fields, to which all the inhabitants were entitled, but the jury was responsible for seeing that no-one took more than their fair share. Both furze (for fuel) and dung were restricted to what a person could gather by hand and 'carry away on their head or shoulders', undoubtedly an effective way of limiting what each person took. At the time of the enclosure the Bailiffs and Burgesses described the poor as 'very numerous and chiefly supplied with fuel from the Heath and Southcombe, not only for their own consumption, but have a right to cut and sell the same, and are in great measure supported thereby.'

The Court also chose the borough officers. These consisted of two Constables, two or three Tythingmen, who were practically assistant constables, and for a time two Aletasters whose duty was to see that the ale and beer (and possibly also the meat and bread) sold within the borough were fit for human consumption, together with two Leather Sealers who were to 'try, search and examine all leather made and exposed for sale within the borough, and to seize all leather not properly tanned'. The Clerks of the Market checked on weights and measures and other market regulations, while the Bellman and

Beadle was appointed to patrol the streets between dusk and dawn and 'to bring to justice all vagrants, nightwalkers and disorderly persons'. He received forty shillings if he performed his duty satisfactorily throughout the year and was issued with a warm coat in the winter months.

Such manorial affairs were conducted largely in the open court presided over by one of the Bailiffs or a steward and with the participation of a jury consisting of leading local inhabitants. The meetings of the common council of the Corporation of Bailiffs and Burgesses were very different. They were indeed a closed corporation with no semblance of democratic election and their meetings were private. They served for life and when a vacancy occurred they chose someone (always a man, of course) to become a new Burgess. Each took an oath to keep the proceedings secret on pain of being expelled and 'utterly spewed out' of the Corporation. The two senior members, the Bailiffs, were chosen from among the members by the process described in the charter. This happened at the annual meeting on the Monday after Michaelmas. It was usual for the retiring Bailiffs to become Chamberlains for the ensuing year and to keep the corporation accounts. Two Sergeants at Mace were appointed to carry the gilded maces on ceremonial occasions[2] and to carry out various other duties on behalf of the Corporation.

The Corporation acted as trustees for several charitable bequests, most important of which was the Henry Cornish Almshouses. From time to time they allocated an almshouse vacant on the death of an inmate to some other widow who met the terms of the bequest. On one occasion a widow was evicted for ungodly behaviour, but what she said or did is not recorded. Cornish had also left money to provide 4d to each of forty other widows in the town and the allocation of 'Cornish's Groats' was an annual item on the Corporation's agenda at Christmas, the minutes listing the names of all the recipients. Other charities provided money annually for two 'decayed tradesmen' and to apprentice a boy from a poor family to some trade.

---

2 There were clearly two maces in use at this time but only one remains today, and that has had a chequered history. Shortly after the Municipal Corporations Act of 1835, which brought the old Corporation to an end, there is evidence for the sale of at least one of the maces. In 1841 Edmund Woodman, a butcher with premises in Spring Street, bequeathed to his nephew William Woodman, '*the silver mace formerly belonging to the Corporation of Chipping Norton and of whom I purchased the same*'. Perhaps they were both sold at the same time. The one now in use was acquired by the Ashmolean Museum who restored it to Chipping Norton Borough Council in the early twentieth century. The other is still missing.

Page from the Corporation minutes, 1728. It includes an entry granting a 'foreigner' freedom to trade in the borough on payment of the customary fees and 'ten shillings to treat the chamber'. Two other people are being appointed Burgesses, which was the normal way of filling vacancies on the Corporation. There were no democratic elections. (Oxfordshire Record Office)

A frequent item at the quarterly meetings was the granting of freedoms. Under one of the original by-laws no-one could practise a trade of any sort within the borough until they had been granted the freedom to do so by the Corporation. It was a rule reminiscent of medieval trade guilds who wished to maintain high standards and to restrict competition, but had probably become more a means of raising money for the Corporation by the eighteenth century. Freedoms were granted on payment of a fee except in the case of a son succeeding his father in which case the fee was waived on production of the father's certificate. Serving an apprenticeship in the town also qualified for a lower rate, but new applicants who were 'foreigners' from some other town paid the full amount – and sometimes more. An entry in the Corporation minutes for 1728 records that at a meeting held at the White Hart William Willcox described as a currier and a foreigner was admitted a freeman of the Borough on payment of five guineas and the accustomed fees, and an additional 'ten shillings to treat the Chamber'. Among those taking up freedoms at this time were some whose names were to become particularly well known, such as William Meades (in 1741), a stone mason whose descendants rebuilt the church tower in the next century and worked on many other buildings, William Hitchman (1759) founder of the town's brewery in Albion Street and Thomas Bliss (1762) clothier, first of the dynasty who built the conspicuous tweed mill. Failure to apply for a freedom was punished under the by-law with a fine, and in 1723 the Town Clerk was instructed to 'prosecute Mr Pool for exercising the trade of a milliner not being a freeman of this Borough'. There was a marked increase in the number of freedoms granted in the latter part of the century, especially in retail trades, suggesting a growth in the town's prosperity.

Other sources of the Corporation's income were the fines and fees imposed in their court of 'pie powder' held during the annual fairs and in the Court of Record held at other times to hear small debt claims. Stallholders and farmers who came from outside the town to fairs and markets also had to pay a toll. Local inhabitants were exempt but 'foreigners' had to pay. The tolls for livestock and corn brought into the town for sale were usually let to the highest bidder who collected them and hoped to make a profit on the deal, while the Corporation was assured of the agreed amount. The amounts varied, however, that for cattle appearing to decline towards the end of the century while the corn toll rose steadily from £8 8s in 1793 to £15 in 1802, perhaps because of wartime prices.

The quarterly meetings of the Corporation might normally have been held in the Guildhall, referred to at that time as the Town Hall, but perhaps because it was in poor repair – described as 'ruinous and dangerous' in 1772[3] – it is clear that on many occasions they preferred to meet in the more congenial surroundings afforded by one of the local inns. Many are named in this connection, among them The Talbot, Bell, Black Boy, King's Head, Unicorn, Blue Boar, Crown and Cushion, Swan, Fox, etc. The favourite, however, was the White Hart, used on numerous occasions. Not only was it probably the largest inn in the town, but the landlord in the 1720s was William Heynes who was one of the Burgesses for many years. It had belonged to Henry Cornish

---

3 In the same year there was a resolution by the Parish Vestry to sell the Guildhall and use the proceeds to build a new town hall and market house. A group of 21 leading citizens was authorised to carry this out, but nothing came of the plan. It is interesting that this came from the Vestry rather than the Corporation. The Guildhall was described as 'belonging to the Inhabitants'. It had been bought for the town by a group of 'feoffees' (see chapter 6) but handed over to the Corporation when the charter was granted. However, some people clearly felt it still belonged to the inhabitants at large and it is interesting that the Vestry saw itself, and not the Corporation, as representing them. When the reformed Borough Council in 1842 finally replaced it with a new Town Hall they felt it necessary to take legal advice first to confirm their right to do so.

and to William Diston in the previous century, so there was a long association with the Bailiffs and Burgesses and it was here that the Bailiff's Feast was
held every year at the time of the Michaelmas meeting. On a few occasions
the Corporation voted that the feast should not be held that year, especially
at the time they were involved in a no doubt expensive petition to Parliament
about the proposed enclosure of the towns fields and commons. The intention
was probably to put the money towards the cost of this action.

The Corporation and the manorial courts were not the only organs of local
government. The Parish meeting or Vestry, as well as its ecclesiastical
powers, was responsible for administering the Poor Law locally. It appointed
Overseers who served for a year and had power to levy a poor rate on the
inhabitants to meet their expenditure on relief for that year. Applicants for
relief had first to prove that they had a 'settlement' in the parish through
birth, apprenticeship or continuous employment for a year, giving rise to
endless 'examinations' to establish their rights. Poor people from another
parish would only be allowed to stay if that parish accepted responsibility for
them. Paupers without a settlement certificate were given a small sum by the
Churchwardens and removed to the next parish as quickly as possible, especially if a woman was pregnant, because her child would become the
responsibility of the parish where it was born, unless the father could be made
responsible. Illegitimate children were therefore a problem and
Churchwardens and JPs spent much time and energy trying to identify
fathers. In 1752 they obtained a bond from Thomas Turner of Cleveley 'for
saving the parish of Chipping Norton harmless from all expenses etc on
account of the birth of a female bastard child which Jane Taylor had latterly
been delivered of and begotten by the said Thomas Turner'. The Overseers
were responsible for assessing and supplying the needs of paupers legally
settled in the parish and their accounts list cash payments to individuals and
families, and sometimes payment for nursing poor people with the smallpox
in the Pest House which was situated at the edge of the town (near what is
now the top of The Leys).

The Rev Edward Redrobe, vicar for nearly forty years from 1683 until his
death in 1720, left £100 in trust to the Minister, Churchwardens and Overseers
to be invested at 5% interest and from the income to provide annually at
Michaelmas four coats and gowns and eight pairs of shoes for four poor men
and four women. The parish got a double benefit from this bequest because
they invested the capital in providing a parish workhouse, thirty-two members
of the Vestry binding themselves to guarantee the payment of £5 a year to the
charity to purchase the coats and shoes. This workhouse was used to provide

basic board and lodging for people who could not otherwise support themselves. For many years the Vestry adopted the system of 'farming' the workhouse to someone who would undertake to run it on their behalf, using an agreed amount from the parish poor rate and making a living for himself out of it. In October 1793 and again in January 1794 they advertised in *Jackson's Oxford Journal* for

> A proper person to farm the poor of the parish of Chipping Norton either by the head or altogether at an annual sum. There is a convenient Workhouse and necessary accommodations. Any person properly recommended who can find employment for the poor may apply to the Overseers of the said parish.

They appointed Visitors to keep an eye on this arrangement, which was obviously open to abuse. An inventory of the contents of the workhouse when it was handed over to a new Keeper lists several spinning wheels, suggesting that there was an attempt to provide work for the inmates so that they could contribute to the costs of running it. It also mentions 'the garden all planted in the Spring', probably another source of work and a means of growing some of their own food. This workhouse was situated in Church Street next to the Grammar School. It remained in use until the reform of the Poor Law in 1834 and in recent times became an attractive private house appropriately named 'Redrobe House'.

The most important event of the century as far as the townspeople were concerned was the enclosure of the open fields and common lands of the parish in 1769–70, and it was in this matter that the Bailiffs and Burgesses stand out as defenders (albeit unsuccessful ones) of the rights and interests of the ordinary people, especially the poorer inhabitants; a rather different image from their usual one of being interested more in their own importance. By the middle of the eighteenth century the centuries-old communal system of agriculture, based on open fields and commons, was fast disappearing in order to make way for more progressive methods of farming. To make this possible individual farmers needed control of their own land arranged not in scattered strips but in larger, enclosed units. Enclosure could only be authorised by an Act of Parliament passed on the petition of the majority of the landowners. The petition submitted by sixteen landowners in Chipping Norton followed the standard format and wording of all such documents arguing that the open fields and commons 'lie greatly intermixed and are of small advantage to the Proprietors and in their present situation are incapable of improvement'. They therefore sought leave to bring in a Bill 'for Inclosing and Dividing the said

Common fields and Commonable Lands'. The petitioners were named as The Earl of Shrewsbury, John Marten Watson, George Tisley, Edward Witts, Robert Fletcher, John Robbins, Thomas Stevley, Thomas Pagett, Thomas Gibbs, William Wilcox, John Insall, John Lock, Samuel Huckvale, William Meades, Joseph Walker and Thomas Watson. Groves Wheeler and Henry Dawkins had also been included with some of the above in the preamble to the petition.

When the details of the Bill were published in Chipping Norton there was an immediate outcry because it proposed to enclose some of the common lands granted to the town by Richard Fitzalan in the thirteenth century. The Bailiffs and Burgesses immediately called a public meeting and a petition against the bill was sent to Parliament, signed by the Bailiffs and Burgesses as lords of the manor and by about two hundred parishioners and principal inhabitants. 'The Case of the Bailiffs and Burgesses' lists these lands and shows the customary use of them in the eighteenth century. Described as Smith Mead, the Sidlings of the Primsdowns as set out by Meerstones, the Vernehill on the north side of the Primsdown, the Brue and Southcombe, they were used as follows:[4]

(i)   The Great Common (150 acres) which was heyned from Candlemass (2nd February) to May Day, and stocked with horses and cows only from May Day to Martinmas (11th November) and with sheep for the remainder of the year.

(ii) The Heath (150 acres) which was open the whole year round for cattle and sheep.

(iii) Southcombe (150 acres) which was open for all of the year, being stocked with horses and cows from Easter to Lammas (1st August) and with sheep for the remainder of the year.

(iv) Vernehill (50 acres) which was opened each year on Whitsun Eve. Every other year all occupiers were allowed to turn on horses and cows from Whitsun to Lammas, but in the second year only occupiers of land had the right to turn on cattle till Martinmas. From then until Candlemas it was sheep common, after which it was heyned.

(v)   Lammas Ground (150 acres of pasture) which was common for horses and cows only from Lammas to Martinmas and for sheep from then on to Candlemas, being closed for hay from Candlemas to Lammas.

(vi) Arable lands in the open fields (1,500 acres) which were then farmed on the four-field system, so that one quarter annually lay fallow in common

---

4 As quoted by Meades.

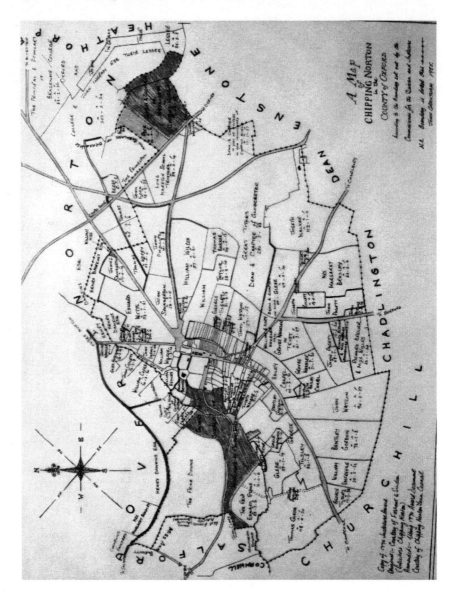

Copy of the Enclosure Map of 1770.
The original map has not survived but this version is based on an early 19th century copy.
It shows the division of land agreed among the landowners in 1770 and the remaining
areas of common land over which the inhabitants had shared rights. (Chipping Norton
Town Council and John Grantham)

and the remainder was sown with grain or pulses and when harvested was common for horses and cattle until All Saints' Day (1st November).

The Case of the Bailiffs and Burgesses stated that at that time the town consisted of about 300 houses. There were about 150 acres of pasture in ancient enclosure. The lands were divided into 74½ yardlands in the open fields.

> The usual stint or custom of stocking the commonable lands with great cattle has been four horses or cows to a yardland, and two to a house, so that the householders have a right to more than two-thirds of the Common Grounds comprised in the said grant, and also to a right of common, as is before mentioned, upon the said other commons called Vernehill, Lammas Ground, and on the Common Field Land. By immemorial custom, every occupier of a house within the town of Chipping Norton has a right of common upon the Premises mentioned in the Grant, as well as the Proprietors of lands, who are very few in number; and as the poor inhabitants were doubtless the objects of Lord Arundel's bounty, they hope they have a right, and that they will be permitted to enjoy the benefit of that Gift in its fullest extent.

But the petition had only a limited success. The Enclosure Award was made in July 1770 and all that remained of Lord Arundel's grant of 500 acres was 124 acres of the Great Common. In addition 74 acres at Southcombe were allotted to the owners and occupiers of houses in Chipping Norton in lieu of their rights over the common fields, and 20 acres to the Bailiffs and Burgesses for the benefit of the poor of the borough. It became the normal practice to put this out to lease and to use the proceeds to buy fuel for the poor because one of the most important rights they had been deprived of was that of collecting fuel on the commons.

The Enclosure Award also commuted the tithes payable by landowners to the rector (the Dean and Chapter of Gloucester) and to the vicar, by allotting land to them according to the agreed value of the great and small tithes. A very large acreage on the east of the town was thus given to the Dean and Chapter. A further large area went to Brasenose College in lieu of the holdings of the former Cold Norton Priory. The rest of the land was laid out in compact fields and divided between the landowners in proportion to their previous holdings in the open fields. They were ordered to enclose their holdings with hedges or fences at their own expense within six months. They had in addition to meet the considerable cost of obtaining the Award and paying the fees and expenses of the Surveyors appointed to measure and apportion the holdings.

The Surveyors also had the power to set out new roads and to re-align old ones and a separate section of their Award specified these. The typically straight lines of the present London, Banbury and Over Norton roads as they leave the Horsefair end of the town were laid out in place of several more winding routes between the furlongs of the open fields and the old path through the Cleeves to Over Norton. Another old road known as the Wool Way crossing the parish from Chadlington towards Rollright was closed except for a short stretch between the Banbury road and the 'road to Birmingham'. All except bridle roads were to be sixty feet wide throughout their length. They were described as the turnpike road from Chipping Norton to Bourton on the Hill, the public roads from Chipping Norton to Banbury, Enstone and Bicester, public roads from the north-west end of Guy's Lane in Over Norton to Long Compton and from Over Norton to Great Rollright, the road from Charlbury to Hook Norton, and from Chapel House to Priory Farm, another public road from 'an ancient lane in Chipping Norton afore-said near the Pest House to Churchill', the roads from Chipping Norton to Burford and Woodstock, from Over Norton to Salford and 'old enclosures in Chipping Norton called the Primsdowns'. The other road concerned was that leading 'from and out of the turnpike road leading from Chipping Norton to Bourton on the Hill to Cornwell ... from Salford to Bourton on the Heath ... from Fernhill into Chipping Norton Great Common as far as the same passeth over the lands of the said Act to be enclosed.'[5]

The Enclosure changed the landscape of Chipping Norton and affected the lives of many people. Farmers and owners who had been able to take advantage of the improved methods it made possible no doubt prospered, especially when the war with France at the end of the century kept wheat prices high. At the other end of the social scale, however, there were those who suffered from those high wheat, and therefore high bread, prices, while their wages remained low and their former common rights were restricted or lost. There were disturbances in several parts of the county in the 1790s and on one occasion wagons carrying wheat belonging to Farmer Atkins of Chipping Norton were attacked and the corn siezed by a crowd of men at Bloxham.

Serving in the county Militia, which was a duty imposed on a number of men selected by ballot from every parish, might have provided a welcome escape from poverty and shortages at home, but not in the sad case of Henry Parish of Chipping Norton. In the same year as the affair at Bloxham, when bread was short and prices high, he was in camp with the Oxfordshire Militia at East Blatchington near Brighton. In spite of inadequate pay, shortages of

5 Quoted by Meades.

flour for bread and resulting high prices, army regulations required that a soldier's pigtail should be dressed with flour. Suspecting that farmers and dealers were restricting supply in order to keep the price high, a number of militiamen attempted to increase the supply and reduce prices by breaking open bakers' shops and ransacking flour mills. They distributed their booty to the crowds and were accused of planning to sell £5,000 worth of flour 'at a fair price' at Lewes market on the following day. Troops sent to deal with them met with strong resistance, and at the subsequent court martial a number of the rioters were sentenced to be flogged, one to transportation to Botany Bay and the ringleaders, Henry Parish of Chipping Norton and Edward Cook of Witney, received the death sentence. This was carried out with brutal formality at Goldstone Bottom, a hollow in the Downs not far from Brighton, with twelve of their fellow rioters forced to form the firing-squad, while the rest of the regiment were made to watch from the surrounding heights. The *Gentleman's Magazine* carried an account which managed to give the occasion an air of aweful, almost religious, solemnity clearly aimed at reassuring readers who might have been horrified at the barbaric ritual:

> After the corporal punishment had been inflicted on offenders of less note, Cook and Parish, the two unfortunate men condemned to die, were brought forward with a strong escort. They walked along the Vale in slow and solemn procession, accompanied by the clergyman who had conscientiously devoted his time to them from the moment the sentence had been made known, and they were fully prepared to meet their fate. Upon approaching the fateful spot, with resignation and religious confidence, they kneeled down upon their coffins with cool and deliberate firmness; when the one who was to drop the signal said to his comrade, 'Are you ready?' Upon the reply being made he dropped a prayer book and the party did their duty at about six yards distance. After this the whole party was ordered to march round the dead bodies.'

An old print in Brighton museum shows the condemned men kneeling on their coffins in front of the firing-party. They were buried in Hove churchyard. Though the riot caused the removal of the prefix 'Royal' from the title of the regiment, it seems to have led to some amelioration of army conditions. There is no record of how the story of his death was received by Henry Parish's family in Chipping Norton.

A notorious but much less serious riot happened in Chipping Norton itself in 1754. The campaigns associated with the parliamentary election of that year aroused strong feelings in the town. There had been no contested election in

The White Hart, the chief inn in the town and favourite venue for meetings of the Corporation in the 18th century. Already a very old building by the time this new front was added in 1724. The inn sign in this photograph is painted on metal and fixed to the wall instead of the more usual position hanging over the pavement. These were probably precautions taken after the earlier sign was burned during the 1754 election riot. (Chipping Norton Museum)

the county since 1710 because the Tories had been unopposed, but in this year the Whigs also put up two candidates.[6] In the previous year there had been demonstrations of support arranged by the rival parties at the annual race meeting held on Chipping Norton Heath and the Tories organised a dinner at the White Hart which was attended by 97 gentlemen all pledged to support the Tory candidates, Wenman and Dashwood. The landlord was William Heynes whose sympathies clearly lay with the Tories. A much smaller number of Whigs met at the Talbot, hosted by a Whig landlord called Wheeler. This

---

6 The Oxfordshire election of 1754 became notorious for the amount of bribery and corruption and the general mayhem associated with the campaign. Buying votes by providing lavish amounts of food and drink for supporters at feasts like those held in Chipping Norton was common practice. Hogarth recorded such a feast in his painting 'An Election Entertainment', which also shows a banner with the slogan 'Give us back our Eleven Days' – a reference to the calendar change of 1752 which was a side issue in this election.

pattern was reversed a year later when, on 1st February, the day of the annual Chipping Norton Feasts, the Whig candidates, Parker and Turner, assembled a huge number of supporters and provided food and drink for them at no less than eight of the town's inns, while some Tories again dined at the White Hart. According to a colourful (and almost certainly exaggerated) report in *Jackson's Oxford Journal* which described the events in the style of a military engagement, the candidates were met outside the town by 400 horsemen, most of whom they alleged to be freeholders (and thus entitled to vote). These divided into three columns and marched into the town in a triumphant procession to the beat of kettledrums. After the meals had been consumed and no doubt many toasts drunk, a group of 'ruffians' hired by the Whigs and the landlord of the Talbot attacked the White Hart where the Tories were dining, smashing windows, trying to break open the gates and succeeding in burning the inn sign. The actual voting at public 'hustings' took place in Oxford in April 1754, accompanied by more outrageous goings on and the two Tory candidates were declared elected. The defeated Whigs contested the result, however; a number of votes were declared invalid and the matter was finally referred to the (Whig) House of Commons who duly declared in favour of their own candidates.

Jackson's Oxford Journal was started at the time of this notorious election but lasted for many years, commenting and carrying advertisements and notices for all kinds of events throughout the county. References to Chipping Norton frequently include mention of the annual race meetings on the Heath.

The spinning and weaving of wool was still carried out in and around Chipping Norton as a cottage industry with much of the work being done by hand in the homes of local people. Some of these were employed by William Fowler when he set up a business based in New Street in 1746. The finishing process, however, required a fulling mill and because there was insufficient water power available to drive one in Chipping Norton he found it necessary to take his cloth to Swinbrook for this stage. It was then brought back to be dried, stretched on racks set up on Rock Hill. In the 1750s Thomas Bliss came to Chipping Norton, the founder of a family business that was to have a considerable effect on the prosperity of the town during the next two centuries. He was born at Chalford, Gloucestershire in 1736, the son of a clothier, but his first occupation in Chipping Norton was as landlord of the Ram Inn. In 1758 he married Ann, the daughter of Thomas Insall of the Crown and Cushion. Ann's marriage settlement was Green Court, Chalford which Thomas Bliss had inherited from his mother. There is some uncertainty about his early involvement in the cloth trade in Chipping Norton. When he was granted the freedom to trade in the borough in 1762 he was described as 'clothier', but he was still landlord of the Ram, and then from 1771–73 of The Swan. It was quite common for people to follow two trades at the same time, especially innkeepers who sometimes found it difficult to make a living out of that alone, and it is likely that Thomas was combining occupations in this way, especially as his clothier's business was still operating as a cottage industry, most of the work being done in people's homes. He became associated with William Fowler but it is not clear whether he worked with him as a partner in the business or simply for him. He seems to have had his own business by 1786, however, when he purchased from Mr Edward Early (the famous blanket maker of Witney) 'a spring loom with three shuttles and gear' for £3 10s. This was almost certainly the early weaving invention known as the 'flying shuttle' which marked the beginning of the industrial revolution in the cotton and woollen industries. Thomas's son William Bliss took over the business in 1790 and carried through the change from cottage industry to factory system, which developed considerably in the next century.

Another person of great significance lived in the town in the second half of the eighteenth century, who is still remembered today for his pioneering contribution to medicine. The Rev Edward Stone had been born in Lacey Green near Princes Risborough and came to live in Chipping Norton in about 1745 because it was conveniently placed between his two clerical livings at Drayton and Bruern. His house was off the Back Lane, close to what is now Hitchman Drive. He was a typical pluralist parson of the period, enjoying the income from Drayton but paying a curate £30 a year to do the work, while he also collected a stipend from what was possibly little more than a sinecure as chaplain to Sir Jonathan Cope in the private chapel of his residence at Bruern Abbey. Cope, who had formerly been one of his students at Wadham College Oxford, had appointed Stone to both places. Not surprisingly Edward Stone seems to have been active in support of his patron's party, the Whigs, in the 1754 election, signing the nomination papers for the Whig candidates Sir Edward Turner and Viscount Parker, and in 1761 he became an Oxfordshire JP.

One result of this sort of clerical lifestyle was that Stone had time to employ his lively intellect on other things and his important work was in the field of

---

7 While the name Aspirin was registered by the firm of Bayer, the drug itself could not be patented because its discovery was due partly to the earlier work of Edward Stone. For this reason it is one of the cheapest drugs today, and one of the most widely used. The world has indeed reaped the benefits as Stone intended.

science. Perhaps because he himself suffered from rheumatism he became interested in treatments for complaints apparently associated with damp places and experimented with willow bark, which also grew in such places and conformed to the current theory that natural cures were often to be found close to the causes of a disease. The slightly bitter taste also reminded him of the conchona bark of Peru, already used as a medicine. He took a sample of willow bark, dried it on a local baker's oven and pounded it to make a powder which was then tested in one of the earliest clinical trials on about fifty people in Chipping Norton who suffered from 'agues' or fevers, gradually increasing the doses and observing the effects. The results were very encouraging and, convinced that he had discovered something of value to many people, he described his experiments in a letter to the President of the Royal Society in 1763. His letter closes with the words: 'I have no other motives for publishing this valuable specific than that it may have a fair and full trial ... and that the world may reap the benefits accruing from it'. What he had in fact discovered was the effect of salicylic acid, which later became the active ingredient of the drug aspirin, eventually produced in 1899.[7]

Edward Stone had an inquiring mind and a wide range of interests. His other academic achievement was the publication in 1761 of a work titled *The Whole Doctrine of Parallaxes*, which included 'an arithmetical and geometrical construction of the transit of Venus over the sun, 6th June 1761'. A second transit was due in 1769 and Stone calculated the best places from which this important phenomenon could be observed. (Important because it allowed an opportunity to make accurate calculations of the size of the sun and its distance from Earth.) His book was reissued in 1768 and was probably taken into account when the government decided to send Captain James Cook to Tahiti in 1769 to observe the second transit. Edward Stone died at Chipping Norton in 1768 and was buried at Horsenden.

A contemporary of Stone in Chipping Norton was the Rev John Thorley, minister of the Presbyterian church in New Street. Before coming to the town he too had served as chaplain to a wealthy patron, Sir William Ashurst, former lord mayor of London, but unlike Stone he served his congregation actively for a remarkable sixty years from 1699 to 1759. He also took an interest in other things and at the age of 73 wrote a book about his hobby of beekeeping which had the backing of almost 800 subscribers before publication. He is credited with developing the use of burning puffballs to quieten bees and inventing a new design of wooden hive.

Thorley had no immediate successor in the Presbyterian church, but in 1775 it was revived as a Baptist congregation largely through the initiative of the Huckvale family of Over Norton. Thomas Bliss was among the founding members, his family in Gloucestershire having Baptist affiliations, and the Rev Thomas Purdy was the first pastor. Also in New Street was a Quaker meeting house, enlarged because of its growing number of members in 1804. The Wesleyan Methodists built a chapel in Distons Lane in 1792.

Chapter 9

Victorian Expansion and Prosperity

Chipping Norton grew and flourished during the nineteenth century, perhaps more than at any other time. Although farming remained important for most of the century industrial and commercial development increasingly underpinned the economy and dominated the life – and the appearance – of this rural market town. Businesses such as Bliss tweed and Hitchman's brewery expanded enormously and became major employers, together with smaller but still important ones like glovemaking and tanning. Many different trades and retail outlets flourished, and by 1855 Chipping Norton had its own branch railway line linking it to the main network. New houses as well as commercial premises were built in many parts of the town, replacing older ones but also adding new ones on the outskirts, especially around West End and The Leys, a new road developed in the 1880s. The two huge tweed mills, the brewery and new buildings like the workhouse, town hall, police station, schools and the premises of the Co-operative Society changed the appearance of the town and signified its growing sense of self-sufficiency and civic pride.

This story is reflected in the growth of the town's population, which more than doubled from 1,812 at the beginning of the century to 4,222 by 1891. In the last decade, however, it fell back to 3,780 by 1901. Such a fall was common in rural areas from the 1880s because of the declining prosperity of agriculture but in Chipping Norton it came rather later as the town was not so dependent on farming.

Gardner's Directory of 1852 lists about 150 tradesmen and women, shopkeepers and professionals serving the town and surrounding district. It is an impressively diverse collection ranging from attorneys like Weston Aplin and

---

1 These two premises are still occupied by banks.

Abram Lindow Rawlinson (who probably built The Elms in Church Lane), to painters and plumbers like George Allcock and William Basket, who was also a 'paper hanger'. There were 20 hotels and inns in the town plus the Royal Hotel at Chapel House, seven grocers and tea dealers, a further eight smaller shops described as 'grocery and sundries dealers', five bakers, five butchers and eleven boot and shoe makers. There were blacksmiths, builders and carpenters; cabinet makers and coach builders; tailors, milliners and dress-makers. The 'miscellaneous' list included Hannah Herbert, straw hat maker, and Thomas Keck a rope maker who used the length of the former burgage plot behind his High Street workshop to stretch out the hemp fibres and twist them into new ropes. The 1851 census shows a flourishing shoemaking industry centered on Finsbury Place near the top of New Street, and run by a man who had been born in Finsbury, London.

There was a Chipping Norton Bank which issued its own notes carrying the names of its partners Corgan, Paget and Matthews. This operated in the early part of the century until local banks were stopped from issuing notes in 1844. At this time property deeds suggest that it was still common practice for house purchases to be financed by loans from private individuals. As local commerce increased, however, larger banks set up branches in Chipping Norton. There was an agency allowing local people to do business with the Stourbridge and Kidderminster Bank by 1834, which operated until taken over by the larger Birmingham and Midland Bank in 1880. This was the bank to which Bliss eventually mortgaged his business. As the Bliss family left the town in 1896 they would perhaps not have enjoyed the sight of the imposing new premises being built by the bank on the lower side of the market place, where the old Borough Arms pub had been demolished to make room for it. On the top side of the market place Gillett's Bank, a long established Banbury firm, also opened a new branch in 1880.

Undoubtedly the most important industrial development was the remark-able growth of the Bliss woollen mills, which became well-known far beyond Chipping Norton for their quality tweeds. From its early beginnings as a cottage industry in the previous century, William Bliss I (there were to be four William Blisses in this century) started the move towards factory production. The work was based on a converted malt house in New Street (the 'Upper Mill') which had been purchased in 1804. Although a horse wheel was installed here to drive machinery it was not fully satisfactory, and Bliss next acquired an old flour mill on the Common and converted it into a watermill for fulling and spinning (the 'Lower Mill'). After being woven the cloth was taken to the fulling mill for cleaning and scouring. Even with the Lower Mill equipped with a water wheel and fulling stocks there was only sufficient water power to operate it for part of the year, and for about four months each year, Henry Scarsbrook the millman who was housed in a cottage at the Lower Mill, had still to take the cloth the ten miles to Swinbrook for fulling.

William had to give up work in 1816 because of ill health, and in this emergency the business was managed by his 14-year-old son Robert and three of his aunts until 1839 when Robert, who had already spent some time in America and married an American wife, finally went to live there permanently. Another brother, the second William, took over and proved himself the most successful of them all, managing the firm until 1883. During that half-century he was responsible for its growth from a turnover of about £10,000 a year to £260,000. The workforce increased in the same period from 11 to over 700. The mills were first enlarged and soon completely rebuilt on a much larger scale and equipped with modern machinery using steam power. The rebuilding of the Lower Mill in 1855 coincided with the construction of the railway, terminating close to it and vastly improving the supply of coal for the steam engine as well as bringing in the 100 bales of wool which the mills were soon to be using every week. It was further enlarged in 1865, forming a substantial building six storeys high and 'one of the most complete mills of the description to be found in any part of the kingdom, filled with the most perfect machinery that could be procured.' *The British Trade Journal* in 1877 featured William Bliss in a series called 'Industrial Celebrities' and describes his mills in Chipping Norton as operating 130 carding engines, 15,000 spindles, and 250 power looms, which produced 25,000 yards of tweed a week. The products were horse clothing, wagon tiltings, army clothing, tweed cloth, shawls and 'railway rugs', which were first produced by this firm. William is said to have spotted a sales opportunity created by the growing popularity of rail travel when he invented the tweed travel rug, a lighter and more fashionable item for use in the unheated railway carriages of those days.

The success of the Bliss Mills, in spite of being situated in a small rural market town far from the main centres of textile manufacture in Lancashire and Yorkshire, owed much to three aspects of William Bliss's management: his initiative in bringing the railway to Chipping Norton and virtually to the door of the mill, his skill in finding and developing a niche market in tweeds (the railway rug story is just one example of this), and his paternalistic management of his workforce. By the standards of his day he was a good employer and his workers achieved high levels of output, perhaps more willingly than in some other Victorian mills. Bliss undoubtedly ran his business well, the *British Trade Journal* article commenting on the 'purity and careful

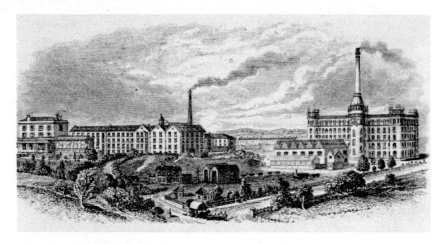

The Bliss industrial empire. A picture designed for William Bliss to impress both clients and competitors and to satisfy his own sense of importance. His grand house on the left of the picture, with its large conservatory and balcony, overlooks both the Upper and Lower Mills with their smoking chimneys suggesting full production, In the foreground locomotives work on the railway he brought to the town. Most impressive of all is the newly rebuilt lower Mill. (Chipping Norton Museum)

selection of the raw material, perfectly adapted machinery and vigilant supervision of the manufacturing process'.

The firm was one of two in Britain awarded a gold medal for good industrial relations at the Paris Exhibition in 1867,[1] and the report contains the following tribute:

> It was on the former of these firms, Messrs Bliss and Sons, that the Emperor of the French was prepared to bestow in 1867 the new order of reward, if Her Majesty's Commissioners could have overcome the difficulties which beset its acceptance by British subjects; and in circumstances on which their claim to distinction was founded, afford sufficiently striking illustration of the inseparable nature of the interests of the work giver and the workman to warrant their being quoted in connection with an Exhibition whose main object was to contribute to the general knowledge of this fact. To their honour, then, let it be recorded that the firm of Messrs Bliss was founded in 1757, and that in 1867 it could be proved that in the 110 years that it had flourished, no dispute had ever occurred between the masters and the 500 hands they had employed; that during that time none of the workmen had joined

---

1 The British Government refused to allow him to receive the award from the Emperor Napoleon III because of political tensions between Britain and France at the time.

Trade Unions, not had Unions had any effect on their wages. There had been no combination; no hands had been allowed to go to the workhouse – families had worked for three generations – the duration of life had been above the average; workmen had saved money and bought life insurances; children had never been employed under 13 years of age, and women employed had not been required to work before breakfast in the winter. School, reading rooms, lectures, concerts, cricket, football, had been liberally promoted. That a gold medal should fall to such a firm and that their tweeds and cloth should be both cheap and excellent, and not suffer in repute from Continental competition cannot excite surprise; but the fact is none the less a source of international gratification, conducive, let us hope, to the promotion and continuance, and the adoption by others of the most remunerative and the only Christian treatment of workpeople by their employers.

While today it might be argued that these apparently contented workers had little alternative to whatever was handed out to them by their employer, it is clear that William Bliss was genuinely proud of his reputation as a good employer (probably even sharing the Christian motive expressed in this citation) and worked hard to retain it through his public works in the town. It is interesting also that at the celebrations for the opening of the new Mill in 1873 the guest of honour spoke at length about Bliss's good relations with his workforce.

In 1872 a severe blow was dealt to the firm when fire destroyed the Lower Mill and killed three men. It happened at night so the casualties were much less than if the workforce had been in the mill. Bliss immediately set about protecting his business and the jobs of his workers by arranging double shifts at the Upper Mill so that orders could still be met. With characteristic determination he also set about rebuilding the Lower Mill, probably borrowing heavily in order to do so. Within the remarkably short time of one year the destroyed building had been rebuilt by J & T David of Banbury, in a style which Bliss intended to enhance his own reputation and the surrounding Cotswold landscape – the imposing structure which still dominates the approach to the town along the Worcester Road. The mill architect George Woodhouse of Bolton was commissioned to design the building and succeeded in producing an efficient and functional industrial building, built on a modular iron-framed and brick-vaulted plan, with a grand stone exterior complete with projecting corner towers and rooftop balustrade. The great chimney became a feature of the front elevation projecting from a cupola and its lower half surrounded by a stairway and rooms making use of the recycled heat from the stack.

It was an expensive project, however, and was soon followed by a period of fierce competition from new industrial rivals – notably the United States and Germany – and a general decline in British industry in the last two decades of the century. A third William Bliss took over the family business in 1883 but the firm never recovered its former prosperity. Tastes were changing from sober Bliss tweeds to brighter Scottish tartans and there was no longer the same demand for Bliss's products. In 1893 the workforce was reduced to 300 and the Upper Mill was closed and put up for sale. Then in 1895 the firm became a limited company, and the Bliss family having lost control withdrew from the business and left Chipping Norton. The Birmingham Bank to whom the company had been mortgaged took over and put A H Dunstan in as Manager on their behalf.

So ended a connection which had lasted for almost 150 years. But William Bliss II in particular had left his mark on the town. A paternalistic employer in the style of Robert Owen, he compensated his workers for low wages and long hours (normal at that time) by caring for their social welfare. In the 1860s and later the mill had a cricket team and sponsored very popular horticultural shows. He provided a library, reading and games room over the Kings Head archway (and later in the upper room next to the Methodist chapel), where debates and discussions were frequently arranged. Good quality cottages in Distons Lane and elsewhere were provided for some of his employees.[2] Nor did he forget the rest of the town, of which he became its greatest benefactor. He was mayor four times, provided land for a cemetery, helping pay for the rebuilding of the Baptist church, contributed towards the provision of a British School and gave donations for the upkeep of the parish churchyard. He was also responsible for the planting of trees beside the roads leading into the town.[3]

The railway benefited both his business and the town when it was built in 1855. Bliss's primary concern in this was to secure a supply of coal for steam power at his mills. He was joined in the enterprise by William Hitchman whose Brewery was another important local industry. The Oxford, Worcester and Wolverhampton railway was under construction in 1845 when the first proposals were made for a linking line which would pass through Chipping

---

2 Perhaps as many as 'a hundred neat cottages and gardens' according to the *British Trade Journal*, which, if true, is far better provision that the rows of back-to-backs available in many mill towns in the north of England.

3 Meades.

Norton on its way towards Banbury, but it was another ten years before such a line was built, and then only as far as Chipping Norton. Bliss successfully argued for the suggested route to be altered slightly so that it terminated close to the Lower Mill, a very convenient arrangement for his business. He and Hitchman probably raised a large amount towards the £26,000 cost and more than half came from the contractor, Sir Samuel Morton Peto. The original station where this line joined the OWW Railway was known as Chipping Norton Junction until 1909 when the name was changed to Kingham. The line was purchased by the OWW Railway Company in 1859 and eventually extended to Banbury in 1877, which had always been the intention. This involved the construction of a tunnel. Stations were provided at Rollright, Hook Norton (where the brewery and ironstone workings benefited), Bloxham and Adderbury on the way to Kings Sutton and Banbury. Private individuals as well as businesses benefited enormously from this, enjoying the opportunity to travel more easily to places like Oxford or Banbury for work or pleasure and, for many of them for the first time, to go much further for family visits or holidays.

Before the railway came there had been reasonable communications with the outside world by road, but it was expensive, slow and often uncomfortable and much of it declined after the coming of the railway. In the middle years of the century the coach service between London and Worcester passed through the centre of the town. The 'Blenheim' and 'Sovereign' coaches provided a daily service in both directions and there was a mail cart to London each evening, to Birmingham every afternoon and to Worcester each morning. Local carriers' carts operated by William Haynes, John Mace, Henry Mason and William Taplin picked up or delivered parcels and goods at various inns in the town and travelled to all the surrounding villages on set days each week. According to *Gardner's Directory* Ward's

Hitchman's Brewery. Another picture designed to advertise the impressive size of the company's premises. With a good deal of artistic licence it shows both the owner's house and company office in West Street and the range of brewery buildings in Albion Street. (Chipping Norton Museum)

wagons and vans carried goods and merchandise to Birmingham, Oxford and Banbury 'almost daily'. Thomas Ward, the proprietor of this business, prospered and built himself a new house at the junction of Spring Street and Over Norton Road.[4] Before doing so, however, he got permission from the borough council, of which he was a member, to alter the line of Spring Street in order to give him a front garden and a more respectable space between his new house and the road. This involved removing some old charity cottages let to elderly people and administered by the council. They were demolished and rebuilt, no doubt affording a better style of accommodation, on the other side of Horsefair with the date and his initials 'TW' on the front. The area around his house became known as 'Ward's corner'. His wagons were kept in Albion street where there was also stabling for the horses.

Other industries in the town included gloving, also well established else-where in the area at centres like Woodstock and Charlbury, which had been present since at least the seventeenth century. Benjamin Bowen who came from Worcester started his business here in about 1829. The skins were processed at the tannery in Distons Lane (suggesting that it was at this date dealing in lighter, cured skins, rather than heavy tanned leather), and much of the sewing was done at home by women in the town and in neighbouring villages. The products were gloves of chamois, leather, cape and sheepskin as well as cowhide leggings. They were sold in Oxford and London and as far afield as Newcastle and Carlisle in the north and around the south and south-east coasts. About the year 1870 a second gloving business was started by John and David Staite at 9 Market Street, and later in a glove factory in Churchill Road.[5]

Hitchman's Brewery was probably the largest employer after Bliss Mill. Founded by James and William Spence Hitchman in 1796, it originally occu-pied premises in West Street, but when James's son William Simkins Hitchman took over after 1830 he expanded the business and developed a much larger site on the upper side of Albion Street (commemorated today by the street name Hitchman Drive). A large poster depicting the works gives the impression that it included steam powered brewery buildings as well as malt-ings, coopers' workshops, wagon sheds and stabling for the drays and heavy horses. W S Hitchman lived in the West Street house in some style (employing a footman in 1851) but also built Kitebrook House for himself as a country residence. He was Chipping Norton's first mayor in 1835. He also owned a

---

4 This house, called Hill Lodge, later became the hospital.

5 Meades.

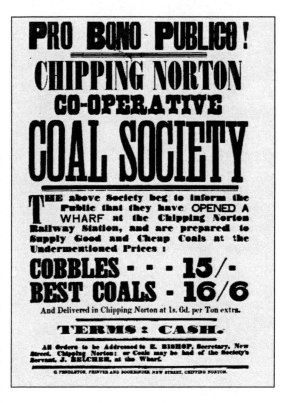

Poster published by the Chipping Norton Cooperative Coal Society in 1866, its first year of trading. (Chipping Norton Museum)

farm, a quarry and a coal merchant's business and leased the town gas works, thus having a hand in several lucrative businesses. His son, another William, eventually sold the business, which became a limited company in 1890.

The concept of co-operative trading took off in a big way in Chipping Norton. Several other Oxfordshire towns had already started co-operative societies, but so far only Banbury's had flourished. In 1866 a group of eight local men purchased a wagon of coal and started the 'Chipping Norton Co-operative Coal Society'. The success of this enterprise encouraged them to open a bakery and a grocery shop in West Street, which were operating by 1869. In 1870 the turnover amounted to over £3,000 and the 143 members received a dividend of 1s in the pound. In 1887 a record 15% dividend was paid. The success of the Society was rapid: membership increased to 1,000 by 1892 and over 2,000 by 1911. Meanwhile the range of its interests was also expanding. Glyme Farm was purchased in 1885 and the Society's newly built shop and headquarters opened in High Street in 1891, setting new standards for Chipping Norton. *The Co-operative News* reported that 'The whole of the premises are supplied with the electric light, the initial turning on of which caused much excitement among the inhabitants, co-operative or otherwise.' The Co-operative movement was not only concerned with trade, however, and Alfred Burden became the first Co-operative Society councillor in the borough election of 1886, although it appears that he did not have the support of all members.

Borough council elections were also a new concept in this century. The old Corporation of Bailiffs and Burgesses established by the charter had been a self-electing body, appointing each new member themselves as vacancies occurred. Once appointed, members could serve for life. Such corporations existed all over the country and were sometimes accused of corruption as well as being resented for being undemocratic. The Municipal Corporations Act of 1835 brought an end to this system. In Chipping Norton a new Borough Council was elected by qualifying ratepayers (men who had paid rates for at least two years). It consisted of sixteen men, twelve of whom, the 'common councillors', had to stand for re-election every three years, while the other four chosen as 'aldermen' served for six years at a time. This body chose one of their number to head the council as 'mayor'. The office of alderman was clearly based on the senior members in the old system, called bailiffs in Chipping Norton. They had also acted as Justices of the Peace in the borough and the new mayor had the same function during his term of office. The Borough Council inherited the lordship of the manor from the old corporation.

One of the first actions of the new council was to build a splendid new town hall in 1842 in keeping with their civic dignity and as a lasting embellishment

The Town Hall about 1850. Built in 1842 it was designed to provide a meeting place in keeping with the civic dignity of the new Borough Council as well as replacing the old market house which provided shelter for farmers' wives and others selling produce on market days. This function was accommodated in the open space beneath the arches, which also housed a weighbridge and a lock-up cell. Some time later the space was enclosed to form another hall on the ground floor. This steel engraving was published by J Liddiard who owned the shop with the rocking horse sign on the right of the picture, where he sold stationary, toys and fancy goods. (Trada, Chipping Norton)

to the town. The old guildhall and other property was sold and the rest of the cost was raised by public subscription with a large donation from J H Langston of Sarsden House. The new town hall was designed by George Repton and being in the Classical style blended well with the Georgian facades of most of the other buildings in the market place. The original design was supported on open arches to accommodate the functions of the 'market house' which used to provide shelter for people selling produce like butter and eggs and which had been demolished to make way for the new hall. It also had a lock-up cell and a weighbridge in this space. A lower hall was created some time later in the century by filling in the arches. This fine building has remained the centre of civic life in the town and a prominent landmark in the market place, almost as much a symbol of Chipping Norton as the town seal which the new council continued to use.

W S Hitchman was the first mayor under the new system. It was normal practice to choose as mayor a leading member of the council, who would also have some standing in the town, and it was not unusual for them to be re-elected several times. William Bliss, not surprisingly, served four terms as mayor. In 1897 when the council decided to commemorate Queen Victoria's diamond jubilee by purchasing a gold chain and ceremonial robes to be worn by future mayors, they were spared the expense through a generous gesture by Albert Brassey of Heythrop Hall, MP for North Oxfordshire, who paid for them and presented them to the town. In return it seemed only appropriate that they should invite him to become mayor, an office he too held for four years, thus becoming the only person to have been mayor without being a member of the council.

This was not the only way in which the people of Chipping Norton showed their enthusiasm for the queen's jubilee. On the day the whole of the upper market place was filled with trestle tables constructed for the occasion and hundreds sat down to a public dinner. The sight was so unusual that it earned a large picture in the *Illustrated London News*. This was followed later in the day by sports and an even larger tea party in Mr Guy's field up Burford Road, when it was reported that close on 5000 adults and children sat down to consume vast quantities of buns, cake and tea produced by an army of ladies who had been working since 9.00 in the morning under the direction of the Town Clerk's wife. The day ended with a giant bonfire fuelled with timber from Brassey's Heythrop Park and several barrels of tar.

From the time of the Enclosure of 1770 various restrictions on the use of the remaining common land were imposed by the Court Baron. The grazing rights (or 'stints' as they became known) had been awarded to the 'owners and occupiers of messuages' but as the population increased and new houses were built, perhaps for people looked on as 'incomers', there was a move to restrict the stints to the number existing in 1770. There was only a limited area of common left and it was felt that it would be inadequate to meet the needs of many more people. Therefore in 1806 it was enacted that 'no house erected upon the waste or new ground' and 'no house divided into tenements' should be entitled to any common, and in 1810 it was plainly stated that 'only those houses standing at the time of the Enclosure' should have any claim to common rights. The stints thus became attached to particular houses and were bought and sold with them. Gradually, however, it became the practice to sell stints separately, for £8 or £10 in the first half of the century, or the grazing could be let. The stints were not separate pieces of land, merely grazing rights, but it occurred to many of the holders that their value would be greatly increased if there was a further enclosure resulting in each stint holder being allotted a piece of the common which could then be enclosed and used for other purposes. The process of enclosure was simpler by now and a new Enclosure Award was made in 1849. The effect of this was to allot 54 roughly half-acre plots on the Great Common close to the Worcester Road and almost as many at Southcombe, which now became private property and in the case of the Worcester Road plots were generally built on in subsequent years. Seventy-five acres of the original common land remained and this was designated Regulated Pasture shared by 53 stint holders (some owning more than one stint out of the total of 85). Field Reeves were to be elected annually to manage the land on behalf of the owners. The Poor's Allotment adjoining the new enclosures at Southcombe remained in the possession of the Council and the rents continued to be used to provide coal for the poorer members of the community. In the 1860s the road across the Common was fenced and the gate at the bottom of New Street and the turnpike gate at the Salford end of the Common, which had prevented cattle straying, were both removed.

The Grammar School was still flourishing in the first half of this century. According to an advertisement of 1835 quoted by Meades 'young gentlemen were carefully instructed in Classical and Mathematical Learning and expeditiously qualified for the Liberal Professions, Government Offices, Commercial and other pursuits' at a charge of eighteen guineas per annum, or fifteen guineas for weekly boarders. French, Drawing, Music and Dancing were of course extra, and tuition in Latin, Mathematics and Land Surveying each cost three guineas per annum. This seems a fairly wide-ranging curriculum for the period. Two free scholars were regularly nominated by the Corporation, who also continued to appoint the Master. Although catering for about fifty pupils in the 1820s, it had seriously declined by 1850 and closed six years later.

By a curious circumstance Charles Stewart Parnell, the great Irish patriot and leader of the Irish Nationalist Party, received some of his education in Chipping Norton in the 1860s, he and his elder brother both attending a small private school run by the vicar, the Rev Alexander Whishaw.[6]

A new National School was built in 1859 on the site of the Grammar School, and managed to take over its endowments. This school, unlike its predecessor, was to be used for 'instruction of children of the labouring, manufacturing and other poor inhabitants of the parish' according to the teaching of the Established Church of England, in keeping with the principles of the National Society. National schools were in consequence usually referred to as 'church schools'. The vicar had considerable control over the school and its teachers, chairing the managers and being responsible for the religious instruction of the children. As in other elementary schools the curriculum consisted of reading, writing and arithmetic and other subjects of a 'practical and elementary' nature, considered suitable for working class pupils. Girls should be taught sewing and needlework, and the elements of the Latin language could be taught to selected boys if the Trustees should require it – which was unlikely at that time to be thought suitable for many of the children this school was intended to cater for. The council, as trustees of the municipal charities, were to have the right to nominate not more than six children of poor inhabitants to be taught free. Other pupils paid small weekly fees fixed by the managers. The managers themselves were chosen from those subscribing more than 20s a year to the running costs of the school.

The British and Foreign School Society, founded in 1808, had started schools mainly for the education of nonconformist children, and in Chipping Norton the first such school was started in the Baptist schoolroom, but in 1854 new premises were provided by converting a large building in New Street,

---

6 Whishaw had been born in St Petersburg, where his wealthy family were prominent in the British community and renowned among the hunting, shooting and fishing fraternity. It was no doubt through connections made there that he was recommended to Parnell's mother by Lord Meath and Lady Londonderry as a suitable tutor for her unruly son. Charles and John Parnell were at Chipping Norton from 1863–65, lodging in a house opposite the vicarage. Their fellow pupils included two other young Irish aristocrats. Charles was unruly and arrogant, but his biographer suggests he was probably educated more consistently in Chipping Norton than ever before. He took an interest in mechanics and was very keen on cricket, which he played at Churchill.

probably with support from the Bliss family. It had separate boys', girls' and infants' departments as was the usual practice, hence the inscription on the front of the building which refers to 'British Schools'. The entrance for girls, whose classroom was on the upper floor, was originally via an open iron stair at the lower end of the building. Even when this had been enclosed, there was no internal connection between the boys' and girls' departments.

Later in the century there was strong rivalry between the established church and the nonconformists, which extended to their schools. The curate of the parish church objected to parents in his congregation sending children to the British School and on more than one occasion made them transfer the children to the National 'church' School. The head teacher of the British School recorded their leaving in his register with the comment 'kidnapped by the Curate'.

In 1837, soon after the building of the first Roman Catholic church in Chipping Norton, Holy Trinity school was opened for children of that denomination as well.

A number of small private schools also existed in the town at various times during the nineteenth century. Lloyd's Collegiate School founded in about 1884 functioned for a time in the rather unlikely location of a room in the Temperance Hotel. A schoolroom which could also serve as an assembly or meeting room is mentioned among the deeds of this property in 1896. Several private schools were for girls, no doubt appealing to the slightly better-off tradesmen who aspired (and could pay for) something better for their daughters. Spinsters who found it a respectable way of earning a living often ran such schools. In the 1830s one run by a Miss Handley took 'parlour boarders'. The Misses Pickess advertised in 1853 for pupils to board and be educated in 'all branches of English Literature, with music, French and other accomplishments'. A school for girls and a kindergarten were later opened at 35 New Street and survived into the twentieth century.

In spite of these private ventures and the much larger National and British schools, there were still not enough places for all the children in the town to attend school. In these circumstances the 1870 Education Act ordered that the ratepayers should elect a School Board with power to levy a rate for the provision a new 'Board School'. Such schools did give religious instruction but were non-denominational and independent of any particular church. This so alarmed the churches in the town, especially the parish church, that the vicar called a public meeting in the town hall to canvass support for a Chipping Norton Education Association which would pool the resources of the Church of England, Non-conformist and Roman Catholic congregations in an attempt to prevent a non-denominational Board School being built. The only way they could hope to do this was to build very cheap extensions to the existing schools and they were advised that this could be done at minimal cost by erecting prefabricated iron buildings. The proposed co-operation between the denominations was remarkable at this time and shows the strength of feeling over this issue. In the end, however, Mr Brassey offered £500 to each of the schools to provide extensions, his only condition being that they were to be built in Cotswold stone and not in iron. The National School extension was built on the corner of Albion Street and Burford Road, while the British School built its in The Green. The Catholics do not appear to have built a new school, and perhaps they declined Mr Brassey's gift – or perhaps he did not include them in it.

One Chipping Norton boy at least in this century went on to university and became an eminent scientist, though we do not know whether his earliest education was at one of the schools in the town. George Percy Darnell Smith was born in 1868 in a house in West Street,[7] the son of Josiah Smith a doctor who himself came from London. He sent his son to University College School in London for his secondary education and George went on to get a degree in botany and zoology at University College itself. For a time he lectured in chemistry and zoology in Bristol and became a Fellow of the Institute of Chemistry, but his most important work was done after he emigrated in 1909 first to New Zealand and then to Australia, where he was appointed Biologist in charge of the newly established Biological Branch of the Sydney Department of Agriculture. Here in 1917 he made a major contribution to international plant pathology by discovering an effective treatment for a serious disease called 'bunt', which was affecting wheat crops throughout the world. His method, using dry copper carbonate, quickly became the standard treatment and significantly increased the average yield per acre in the major wheat producing countries.

Chipping Norton parish church was extensively repaired and 'restored' in the nineteenth century. First came the rebuilding of the tower in 1823. The decision to undertake such a considerable amount of work suggests that the tower must have been in a dangerous condition. It was claimed at the time that the new tower would be similar to the old one, but it differs in two notice-able respects. The buttresses on the original tower extended to the level of the

---

7 The house next to the King's Arms. In his later professional life he chose to hyphenate his name to George Darnell-Smith, which no doubt sounded more impressive than mere Smith.

battlements, whereas on the new one they stop lower down. On the south side of the new tower there is also a recess clearly intended for a clock. Unfortunately no clock was provided, probably because the money ran out, and the recess is still empty today. On the inside of the battlements of the new tower the name of Meades the stonemason is carved, together with later initials and outlines of shoes scratched into the lead, in keeping with an old superstition for which there is evidence on several other church towers.

In 1841 box pews were installed and a second gallery was built on the south wall. Many of the pews would have been reserved for the use of families and individuals who paid rent for them. The new gallery no doubt seated less 'respectable' members of the congregation. Like the older west gallery, it had a separate entrance by means of an external stair to the left of the porch and main doorway. The front of the north aisle was used by the Dawkins family of Over Norton House. Their mausoleum and memorials were erected at the far end of this aisle and it was often referred to as the 'Over Norton aisle'. Since at least the seventeenth century the parish had elected a third churchwarden, instead of the more usual two, known as the Over Norton warden.

Later in the century there were further alterations to the main structure and to the interior.[8] Plaster was scraped from the walls – sadly destroying all trace of the medieval wall paintings which would almost certainly have adorned them – and those which were still visible on the roof were removed at the same time. (Brewer writing in the early years of the century described the nave roof as being 'rudely carved with numerous interspersed stars and other embellishments'). The screen with its list of benefactors was removed from the chancel. The further restoration of the 1870s involved the dismantling of both galleries and replacement of the box pews by open ones which now became free. The floors of the chancel and sanctuary were raised, elevating the altar above the level of the congregation in the nave, perhaps influenced by the Ritualist movement. The whole floor of the church was repaved with mosaic tiles. Sadly this involved removing the medieval brasses originally set in stone memorial slabs on the floor. The brasses were prized off them and stored carelessly in a chest. A number disappeared before the remaining ones were rescued by a later vicar, the Rev Godfrey Littledale, mounted on oak boards and displayed on the north wall of the St John the Baptist chapel. The stone slabs which had covered the greater part of the chancel floor were sold to a

8 The following description of the restoration and the building of other churches in the town is taken largely from Meades with some additions.

local mason and a few of them may still be visible where he placed them, inscription uppermost, at the entrance to certain cottages. An earlier suggestion that the chancel steps should be purchased by the Council for use in repairing those at the entrance to the Town Hall steps had been rejected. A cottage in Distons Lane has what appears to be a corbel head built into the wall, and it also has part of the old font and what is apparently a holy water stoup.[9]

One important detail, however, was discovered through the scraping of the limewashed walls. When plaster was being chipped away from the pillar on the north side of the chancel arch it became clear that it was not solid, and that the fluted effect was due to ropes dipped in cement. When this and the plaster were removed the original pillar and three niches with pedestals that once carried statues of saints were revealed. These had been surmounted by stone canopies, which were eventually restored. It is almost certain that this fragment is all that remains of an important chantry chapel, probably that of the Trinity Guild, demolished soon after 1549. Burford church has a surviving chapel in the same position which gives a good impression of what this one may have looked like.[10] The discovery of the niches caused tremendous discussion. At the Easter Vestry Mr Bliss advocated restoring the 'shrine' but thought that the replacing of statues 'could not be tolerated'. He offered £25 towards the cost of making the present pulpit in front of the niches. An even hotter controversy was created by the discovery of the pre-Reformation stone altar slab still in the vestry. It would have been replaced by a wooden communion table soon after 1549 as part of the Protestant reforms, and the proposal of a ritualistic curate in the 1880s that it should now be restored as an altar split the congregation in a bitter dispute between 'high' and 'low' church parties.[11] The work was eventually completed at a cost of over £4,000, leaving the church looking very different, but at least in sound condition. By 1881 the churchyard, enclosed early in the century and later enlarged (on which occasion the old pound had been taken in) was too small for the needs of the community, and so William Bliss persuaded the Field Reeves to sell part of

---

9 These things were visible at the time of Meade's first writing her *History*.

10 There is no convincing evidence to support the suggestion made at the time that this chapel, or for that matter the nave of the church, was built by John Ashfield of Heythrop because a small stone shield bearing his arms was also found during the restoration work.

11 Col. Dawkins of Over Norton lead the 'low' party and evicted one of his tenants from a cottage for voting with the ritualists who wanted to restore the altar.

the Regulated Pasture near Primsdown which he then presented to the town for use as a cemetery.

The Baptist meeting house which had been built in 1733, was greatly enlarged in 1817, and then in 1862 the present church was built. The Rev William Gray, who was pastor from 1809 to 1825, turned his house into an academy for training young men, and reported that religion flourished in the town and surrounding villages. In 1852 the pastor was the Rev Thomas Bliss.

The first Methodist superintendent in Chipping Norton, the Rev James Sydserff, was appointed in 1813, and in 1846 the Rev James Rathbone and William Bamford were appointed to the circuit which by then had sixteen chapels. Services were held in the chapel in Distons Lane until the present church was built in West Street. In 1871 the Primitive Methodists, who had been worshipping in a converted barn behind 4 Market Street, bought the old chapel in Distons Lane.

During the three centuries or more since the Reformation there is little information about Roman Catholicism in Chipping Norton. The Rev Edward Redrobe (1683–1721) stated that there were no 'Popish recusants' in the town. In 1738 the Rev R Eaton's returns gave seven Papist families in the parish but by 1774 the number had decreased. The trend was apparently reversed between then and the first quarter of the nineteenth century, though till after the passing of the Catholic Emancipation Act in 1829 there could be no Catholic church in the town. The Catholic Earl of Shrewsbury, who lived in Heythrop Hall, obtained a special licence to build a church in his park in 1821 and after a fire at the hall ten years later a new church was built in Chipping Norton at the instigation of Father Hefferman. This was Holy Trinity Church which was opened in 1836. The fifteenth Earl of Shrewsbury is buried in the crypt. The presbytery is attached to the church and later a small convent was built in the grounds together with a school run by the nuns. The parish covered the area from Shipton under Wychwood to Hook Norton.

Caring for the poor which had once been chiefly a religious duty had since the sixteenth century become the responsibility of the parish Overseers and Churchwardens, but in 1834 the Poor Law Amendment Act set up new authorities formed by linking several parishes together and imposing a much harsher test for recipients of poor relief. Chipping Norton became the head-quarters of one of these Poor Law Unions. The old parish workhouse in Church Street was sold and replaced by a much larger and more forbidding, prison-like building on the London Road. This was built on an approved pattern designed by the architect George Wilkinson of Witney, who came to specialise in building workhouses. The imposing front block contained living accommodation for the Workhouse Master and a boardroom for meetings of the new Poor Law Guardians. Behind it was the workhouse itself with basic accommodation for 230 inmates in three-storey wings radiating out from a central tower, with exercise yards between the wings. The same plan was used for prisons. At the rear was a quarry where able-bodied paupers were set to work on stone breaking.[12] There was also a chapel designed by G E Street,[13] with low benches in the front rows for workhouse children. The government's declared policy was to deter people from seeking poor relief by making it available only to those who were desperate enough to go into the workhouse, and conditions inside it were to be worse than those of the poorest labourer outside. The diet was laid down on similar lines to that in prisons and only slightly more generous. Men and women, including husbands and wives, were separated. The harshness of the regime was gradually lessened towards the end of the century but it is not surprising that these workhouses were known as 'Bastilles' and poor people, especially the elderly, dreaded entering, or even worse ending their days there. Chipping Norton Union Workhouse contained 131 inmates in 1850, who were maintained at a cost of £7 0s 3½d per person per year, which included food and clothing.

The 1870s saw the provision of a more efficient fire service and the beginnings of a piped water supply. There had been serious cholera epidemics in Oxford and other towns earlier in the century and in 1875 two people in Chipping Norton died of typhoid fever. By this time it was recognised that such infections were caused by impure drinking water and inadequate sewerage systems, although the scientific reasons were not fully understood. A clean water supply was eventually installed, though Bliss fell out with the borough council because they were unwilling to accept his proposals for the scheme. The fire which destroyed Bliss's Lower Mill was the main incentive for providing a new and better horse-drawn fire engine in 1878. This was housed in a newly constructed 'engine house' in Burford Road and could be summoned in an emergency by loud ringing of the bell on top of the town hall. A rope for the purpose hung down the lower side of the building.

There were changes too in the policing of the town. The following presentment was made by the jury of the Court Leet in 1815:

---

12 The stone was used for repairing roads. In 1882 when the new cemetery was being laid out it was agreed that 'as much broken stone as could be had from the Workhouse should be used for the footpaths. The men to be employed to break a further quantity'.
13 Perhaps 'on the back of an envelope' as someone recently commented! It was of very plain design.

The jury having noticed with concern the assemblage of persons at the corners of New Street and Church Street on Sabbath Days, respectfully submit the same to the most serious consideration of the magistrates; and also with much deeper concern they notice the increasing evil arising from the number of lewd and base girls that frequent the streets in the evening, which they consider destructive of good morals, and also submit the same to the most serious consideration of the Magistrates.

In 1821 it was ordered:

That the Constables, Tythingmen and all other Peace Officers are desired to be very diligent in dispersing all manner of disorderly persons who assemble themselves at the corners of New Street and Church Street, and all other places within this Borough, particularly on the Lord's Day; and to take such persons who refuse to disperse when ordered before one of the Magistrates.

That all victuallers within this Borough are commanded not to suffer any profuse drinking, tippling or disorderly persons in their houses, particularly on the Lord's Day, and that no beer or liquors be drawn during Divine Service on that day.

The parish stocks which formerly stood at the bottom of Burford Road disappeared in about 1845 and it was necessary a few years later to fetch stocks from Oxford for the punishment of a barber, the last man to be so punished.

All the above examples illustrate a medieval style of law enforcement, but one of the provisions of the 1835 Municipal Corporations Act was that councils could raise rates for lighting, paving and watching (i.e. policing) the streets. A Watch Committee was set up in Chipping Norton and a new type of professional policeman employed to replace the old unpaid parish constables. Rather than appoint a local man who might not be impartial, they wrote to the Commissioner of Peel's recently formed Metropolitan Police and asked him to nominate two suitable officers who were 'strangers to the borough'. On his recommendation the Council appointed Sgt Charles Knott and Constable Barnes. These men were uniformed and equipped with truncheons, handcuffs (with a spare set of keys), lanterns, and rather surprisingly armed with cutlasses. This was a total contrast to the image of an old-style parish constable and while property owners (who originally subscribed towards the cost of policing) undoubtedly felt secure at the sight of such well equipped officers, not all of the ordinary inhabitants welcomed their appearance or the authority they sought to impose. There were occasional attacks on them, such as an 'affray' at the White Hart when one of the officers had his uniform torn, and several complaints against them, some of which the committee felt were partially justified, and cautioned the officers not to frequent public houses. However, these tensions between the inhabitants and the new professional policemen came to a head seriously in November 1845 when Sgt Knott was called to the Bell in West Street one night where two men were fighting over an accusation of theft of some horse fodder in the stables at the back of the inn. According to the report in the *Oxfordshire Weekly News* at the time of the subsequent trial, Knott immediately decided to arrest the accused man, called Slatter, and in doing so hit him across the head with his truncheon and was about to strike him again when the onlookers persuaded him not to. Slatter was taken away and locked up in the cell beneath the new Town Hall for the night, but was found dead in the morning. As soon as the story got out a large and menacing crowd gathered in the Market Place, shouting for Knott, who had gone into hiding. The Mayor appealed for calm but the riot went on into the next day and a note in the Council minute book on Friday evening at 6 pm records that because only a few councillors came to the Town Hall 'and a riot of a serious nature' was continuing outside, their meeting was not held. A troop of the Queen's Own Oxfordshire Yeomanry was dispatched by the Lord Lieutenant 'in aid of the civil power', and after an inquest established that Slatter had indeed died from the blow, Knott was arrested and escorted by the soldiers (for his own safety) to Oxford Gaol. He was eventually tried and acquitted on the rather doubtful grounds that the unfortunate Slatter had an unusually thin skull. Sgt. Knott's replacement was a constable who seems gradually to have been accepted by the locals. However, as soon as a County Police force was established in 1856, the Council readily agreed to hand over responsibility for the borough to Oxford, and a piece of land was purchased for the building of a police station at the bottom of the London and Banbury roads.

There had been agricultural riots in North Oxfordshire in the 1830s when labourers felt their jobs were being threatened by the new threshing machines, and forty years later in 1872–73 fresh trouble broke out in the Chipping Norton area. The centre of the disturbance in May 1873 was Ascott-under-Wychwood, where a number of men who had joined Joseph Arch's new Agricultural Labourers' Union were refused a wage increase by farmer Hambidge of Crown Farm, and went on strike. After three weeks Hambidge brought in two young lads from Ramsden to do the work of these men. A noisy group of women in support of the men met these two and tried to stop them proceeding with the work by a mixture of threats and persuasion.

Hambidge called in the local police and the women were ordered to appear before the magistrates at Chipping Norton. Here Hambidge pressed his charges and the two local clergymen who sat on the Bench that day sent sixteen of the women to prison, seven of them for ten days and nine for seven days, all with hard labour. Such was the effect of the sentence that both *The Times* and *The Daily News* sent down special correspondents and *The Times* of 26th May 1873 carried the following report:

> The labouring population were astounded when they heard the sentence, but they bore it quietly until about nine at night, when the 'roughs' of the neighbourhood, in which there is a manufactory,[14] assembled in considerable force. Then after much shouting, an onslaught was made on the police station; the windows and the door were broken and some of the tiles were stripped off the roof. Police Superintendent Larkin and his men are admitted to have acted with great forbearance, but the Superintendent thought it advisable to telegraph for assistance to Oxford. On receipt of his telegram Inspector Yates, with a force of police, started in a drag and four. So riotous was the aspect of Chipping Norton that it was not deemed safe to keep the women there until the time at which the first train leaves, and in the small hours they were driven in the brake the whole distance to Oxford, where at six in the morning they were locked up in the County Gaol. Petitions to the Home Secretary are spoken of in the district, and so threatening is the attitude of the villagers that on Saturday [i.e. three days after the trial] police were again despatched from Oxford.

The publicity attracted by the events turned this local dispute into a national issue. Questions were asked in Parliament, and the Duke of Marlborough (Lord Lieutenant of Oxfordshire and responsible for the magistrates) received a rather pointed letter from the Lord Chancellor making clear his view that the unwarranted severity of the sentences had damaged respect for law. When the women were released the Union made the most of the propaganda opportunity, meeting them at the prison gate and bringing them

---

14 William Bliss, stung by this obvious reference to his mill, wrote an indignant letter to *The Times* protesting that none of his employees had taken part in the affair except as onlookers, 'and further that at my request they left the scene of the disturbance and quietly dispersed to their homes'. He also claimed that the extent of the damage had been exaggerated. It was typical of the pride he felt in the workers at his mill, and in the town that he probably felt was his too.

Chipping Norton in the 1890s. Most of the built-up part of the town at the end of the 19th century is included on this map, apart from The Leys and the Lower Bliss Mill and station. The Upper Mill and Hitchman's Brewery are prominently marked. It shows the buildings at the top of New Street and on Lower Side which were to be demolished in the 20th century to increase traffic flow. The historic shape of the medieval market place has survived with most of its narrow burgage plots and back lane, while the castle site and church stand slightly apart occupying the older village centre. (Ordnance Survey map. Centre for Oxfordshire Studies)

back in style to Chipping Norton, where Joseph Arch himself addressed a crowd of two thousand people gathered in the market place. This affair was instrumental in bringing about the repeal of the law banning peaceful picketing, and clergymen were less likely to be appointed to the magisterial bench.

Much happier crowds gathered in the market place for the 'Mop' Fair held each autumn. This was an important hiring fair as well as an annual entertainment. It's name, common to several towns, derived from the custom of people waiting to be hired for work identifying their trade by easily recognisable symbols. Just as shepherds carried a crook, so domestic servants carried a mop, and this must have been one of the main occupations catered for, so giving the name to the fair. Held on the Wednesday before the 11th October, it was followed a fortnight later by another fair called the 'Runaway Mop' giving applicants and employers a second chance. Even those who had hired someone or been hired at the first fair were permitted to break the contract in the first ten days and try again at the Runaway Mop. Both fairs, like all others, were also occasions for fun and entertainment.

The hotels and inns around the market place were no doubt crowded and busy on fair days, but the temperance movement was also active in the town and in the 1880s and 1890s alternative refreshment was offered by the Temperance Hotel at 9 High Street. The ubiquitous William Bliss was chairman of the directors of the Chipping Norton Temperance Hotel and Restaurant Company Ltd who owned it. The main public room, still called the 'bar parlour', was equipped with 90 cups and saucers instead of beer glasses but did contain six iron spittoons. There were three sitting rooms and a 'Bagatelle room' for those seeking entertainment. The bedrooms ranged from the front bedroom with two French bedsteads (one with a spring mattress), to the three attic rooms each with an 'iron stump bedstead with straw paliass'.

Chapter 10

The Twentieth Century

Early in the new century the good relations between managers and employees for which the Bliss mills had been renowned were shattered by a bitter strike which broke out in 1913. Average wages paid in Oxfordshire were lower than in almost every other part of England at this time. There had been some improvement for agricultural workers, and considerably more for those in large industrial cities but for men and women working in small factories in rural areas, where wages were about a third lower, it remained to be seen whether they could organise themselves into unions and exert the same pressure on employers. In the Bliss Mill in 1913 the eighteen year-old Miss Grantham was paid 4s for a 55-hour week working 6 am to 6 pm. Unskilled adult workers could earn up to 10s 6d and skilled workers 15s to £1. The paternalistic approach of the Bliss family in the previous century, and their genuine concern for the welfare of their workers, had gone some way to compensate for low wages, but expectations were changing.

The management of the mill had also changed. When the last Bliss went bankrupt and was forced to sell the business, the new manager on behalf of the Birmingham Banking Company was A H Dunstan. In spite of the increasingly difficult times he continued the modernisation of the firm and oversaw the installation of electric lighting in 1904 and electrical machinery by 1910. However, it is likely that there was still much resentment at the change of management and many employees seem to have strongly disliked him. By 1913 there was also growing dissatisfaction with the wages and the conditions of work. Inspired by the success of a union branch at Early's in Witney, which achieved recognition and an increase in wages for the blanket workers in 1912, a branch of the Workers' Union was formed at Bliss Mill in November 1913 with some 200 members. The management countered by proposing the formation of an 'employees association', unconnected with any national trade union, with representatives elected by the employees to frame rules and confer with the managers on matters affecting their welfare. This was rejected

Solidarity on the Town Hall steps. Members of the Workers Union on strike in 1913.
(Chipping Norton Museum)

because of the stipulation that workers should not become members of any
other union, thus greatly weakening their bargaining position. Three men, all
Workers' Union members, were dismissed by Dunstan on the grounds that it
was necessary to reduce numbers because of poor trade. Not surprisingly the
workers regarded this as provocative move against their organisation and their
right to join a trade union and, on Dunstan's refusal to re-instate the three
men, a strike was declared on the 18th December.

The strike was considered important by the Union, and to trade unionism
generally as a test of its strength in rural areas. The number on strike at the
outset was 280, with 150 non-strikers still at work. A strike committee was
formed with headquarters at The Fox Hotel[1] and an appeal made for funds to
help the strikers' wives and children. There was considerable sympathy for
their cause, sometimes from unexpected quarters. The Christmas Day collection at the parish church was given to the fund for the women and children
and a collection was made among sympathetic tradesmen and others in the
town. The Co-operative Society gave £10, followed by a further £20 in
January, and the Old Elm Tree Lodge of Oddfellows donated £10 from their
distress fund. Even the Bishop of Oxford sent a donation and wrote a letter to
the *Oxfordshire Weekly News* expressing the view that 'workers of all grades

---

1 They also used the Temperance Hotel, perhaps remembering William Bliss's
connection with it.

should be encouraged to combine freely in Trade Unions with a view to collective bargaining.[2] Less surprising perhaps was the support given by members of Ruskin College, Oxford, who raised funds and put on entertainments for the strikers at The Fox to keep their spirits up. Several Oxford tutors wrote in support of the strike, notably the eminent historians G D H Cole and G N Clark and the classicist Gilbert Murray. There was also active support from Julia Varley and George Dallas, professional organisers from the Workers' Union. The initial strike pay issued by the Union was: married men 10s with 1s for each dependant; married women 8s with 1s for each dependant; single men 7s, unless they were the only wage earner in the house, in which case they received the same as married men. Single girls received 5s 6d. In January some of the strikers staged a march to London, publicising their cause and collecting donations for their fund.

In a small, tightly-knit community such as Chipping Norton, very strong feelings were aroused between the striking families and those who remained loyal to the management and continued to work. Even those not directly involved were caught up in the tensions. As the strike continued through the early months of 1914, there were fierce arguments and occasional fights. The strikers organised collections and sometimes noisy processions through the streets. On one occasion a gang of them left The Fox late at night and marched through the market place then down Spring Street, New Street, past Dunstan's house, and some went on to The Leys where a number of mill foremen lived. They shouted abuse and threw stones smashing the windows of several houses belonging to 'blacklegs'.[3] They were followed in the dark streets by the local police sergeant who did not attempt to interfere, but noted the identities of the ringleaders, who were later brought before the magistrates.

This was one of a succession of cases tried by the local magistrates, meeting in the Town Hall, surrounded by crowds from both sides of the dispute who couldn't get into the court, waiting on the steps to hear the outcome. Tensions ran high, and on one occasion a respectable member of the local establishment and outspoken critic of the strike was involved in a scuffle with a younger woman striker in the crowd, and was accused of hitting her. In this atmosphere fairly trivial cases became blown up into huge issues (and it was

---

2 The Rt Rev Charles Gore, previously the first Bishop of Birmingham, also noted for his opposition to the use of concentration camps by the British in the Boer War and support for Lloyd George's social reforms in the 1909 'People's Budget'.

3 It was said that these families in The Leys slept in their back bedrooms for years after this night.

in the Union's interest to encourage this). The magistrates themselves were suspected of bias against the strikers and in response requested members of the Bench from outside the town to try cases.[4]

Those still working had to make their way to the mill every morning through vociferous crowds of pickets, and the two local policemen were unable to keep order. Consequently fifty extra police were drafted in to live in Chipping Norton for several months and escort the workers to and from the mill each day. Even this did not prevent the occasional assault. In February Fred Shepherd, a youth in his late teens, was accused of kicking one of the policemen as they escorted the workers down New Street. In court he vehemently denied the charge but was sent to prison for a month when he refused to pay the £5 fine. On the day he was admitted to Oxford gaol another striker, Annie Cooper of Spring Street, was being released after serving her 14-day sentence for a minor assault on one of the workers. She had leant over the fence at the mill and grabbed hold of a man's jacket, pulling him off the lowest rungs of a ladder as he was going up to do some maintenance work. Mrs Cooper was found guilty of assault and given the option of a £5 fine or fourteen days in prison, but urged on by her union colleagues she chose prison.[5] Both her case and that of Shepherd were reported in the national press and questions were asked in Parliament by the local Liberal MP, Eustace Fiennes. For Fred Shepherd this lead to an official pardon when it transpired that the person who had actually kicked the policeman had been a Ruskin College student. On Annie Cooper's return to Chipping Norton after her release she was met at the station and carried triumphantly up into the town on a cart pulled by strikers and accompanied by the 'All Union Band'. That evening the Town Hall was packed for a huge reception in her honour. Among the speakers were Mrs Varley and C E M (later professor) Joad of Oxford. Mrs Cooper was presented with a silver teapot suitably inscribed in memory of her ordeal suffered in the cause of the strikers.

In spite of these high points, the strike dragged on into the summer without much sign of a settlement and the hardship suffered by families without work began to wear down their resolve. Some drifted back to the mill while others left the town to seek employment elsewhere. 160 remained on strike until June 1914. The outbreak of the First World War finally brought the affair to an end

---

4 The Mayor was a magistrate by reason of his office and the Town Clerk acted as Clerk to the Magistrates. J S Hall, deputy manager at the mill, who testified against Annie Cooper, had been a councillor until November 1913. The composition of magistrates' benches at that time did not reassure working men who appeared before them.

Some of the extra police drafted in to keep the peace between strikers and non-strikers during the dispute at the Bliss Mill. Their main duty was to escort non-strikers to and from work every day. (Chipping Norton Museum)

as strikers either joined up or returned to jobs at the mill making uniforms – at piece rates much higher than their former wages. Miss Grantham who had left the town with others to find work in Rochdale, now returned to earn 10*s* for each 25 yard length of khaki cloth, usually weaving two in a week. However, there were still 50 unemployed dependent on the Workers' Distress Committee.

The strike played its part in the growth of the trade union movement in Oxfordshire, encouraging the formation of other union branches, and in the words of the *New Statesman* (22nd April 1914) 'providing a valuable object lesson of labour solidarity for the rural workers of the Cotswolds'. At the Bliss Mill, however, no union branch was recognised until 1945. In the local community the strike left a legacy of bitterness which persisted for many years.[6] A H Dunstan bought the mill from the Birmingham Bank in 1917, but sold it three years later to Fox Brothers of Wellington in Somerset, with whom the Blisses had been trading since 1840.

The First World War caused less disruption than the Second to daily life

---

5 Those urging her on apparently included her husband, who is said to have shouted from the balcony 'you go to prison my girl'!

6 In the late 1960s there were still said to be families who did not speak to each other because they had been on opposite sides in the strike half a century before.

for people in Chipping Norton, but cost many more lives. 105 husbands, sons and brothers from local families died, sometimes two or three from the same family. Typical among these tragedies was Able Seaman Frederick Hake who drowned with many others when his cruiser HMS Black Prince was sunk in the battle of Jutland. He had come to Chipping Norton as one of the policemen drafted in to keep order during the Bliss strike. He met and married a local girl, Edith Stanley, in 1915 but was killed only six months later. Herbert Simms was the son of a well-known Chipping Norton family of watchmakers with a shop in the High Street and his father was mayor of the borough three times. Herbert was passionate about aeroplanes and even attempted to build a bicycle-powered glider which he tested by pedalling furiously but unsuccessfully down Over Norton Road. He learnt to fly while working for A V Roe and after a spell in the Greek Naval Flying Corps joined the Royal Naval Air Service in England in 1915 as a pilot, earning high praise from his commanding officer for his skill and leadership. He was shot down over the North Sea in 1916 and buried in Chipping Norton cemetery with full military honours. Mowbray Meades had grown up in Chipping Norton in the 1880s and '90s. He went to the British School and got his first job as a junior clerk in the Co-op office. In 1909 he married Milly Lambert from Churchill and by the time war broke out they were living in London with their two little girls.[7] In 1916 while in France where his elder brother William had recently been killed at the Somme, he heard of the birth of a third daughter whom he was only to see during brief spells of leave, one after being wounded and sent back to hospital in England. Returning to the front, he was taken prisoner in 1918 and died of pneumonia in the prison camp only four months before the war ended.

When the First War ended in 1918 a memorial was put up in the parish church bearing the names of the local men who had died. Some time before the war Mr A P Walford of Over Norton, together with Albert Brassey of Heythrop had come up with a plan to provide Chipping Norton with a cottage hospital. The war had intervened and Brassey himself died before it was over, but his family agreed to fulfil his wishes. In 1919 this plan was linked with the idea of finding a way to commemorate the men who had died in the war, in addition to listing their names in the church. The concept of a war memorial hospital was seized upon with enthusiasm at a public meeting in the Town Hall in February of that year chaired by the mayor, Thomas Mace. Mr Walford had agreed to give the large house known as 'Hill Lodge' at the junc-

---

7 The eldest of whom was Eileen, author of *The History of Chipping Norton.*

tion of Over Norton Road and Spring Street for the purpose, as it had already been used as a hospital for officers run by volunteers during the war. He and Captain Brassey (Albert's son) would give £3,000 to equip it, and it was estimated that a further £9,000 would need to be invested to meet the running costs. Dr O'Kelly strongly supported the plan on the grounds that sending patients to the Radcliffe Infirmary in Oxford by motor car was often 'a great risk to life'. The money was raised in a short time and the Chipping Norton and District War Memorial Hospital was opened in 1920 with 16 beds and one private ward. In its first year 124 in-patients and 193 out-patients were treated.

Apart from a 30s maternity grant, hospital treatment was not free, and the charges at Chipping Norton were 5s per week in the general ward, or £1 1s for maternity cases, or 'such sum as the committee may decide'. A popular way of meeting the cost for most people was to join the Radcliffe and Associated Hospitals Contributory Scheme, paying 2d a week. There were all sorts of problems in the early years caused by faulty equipment, shortage of staff, leaking roofs, etc., but all were overcome by the determined efforts of the matron, Miss S Brooke-McColl, and the unfailing support of the local community. Fund-raising for the hospital became part of the life of the town, from the annual Hospital Saturday carnival to Egg Day held in May each year, when people contributed sufficient eggs to be preserved in isinglass and used to supplement the patient's meals for the rest of the year.[8] Over the years new facilities were added: a properly equipped operating theatre in 1923 (although minor operations had been carried out before this), a new X-Ray room in 1926 and a maternity ward in 1929. For all of these the capital was raised through donations and fundraising in the town.

The 1939–45 War put a considerable strain on the hospital mainly through shortages of staff, and increasing costs made the situation so bad that the general wards were closed for several months in late 1945. Voluntary support from the town and district was still willingly and generously given but it was becoming less and less adequate to meet the rapidly rising cost of running a hospital. Like other local hospitals it was saved by the National Health Service in 1948, when it was taken over by the state and health care became free. The take over, really a rescue, was greeted with mixed feelings in the local community at the time, many fearing it would no longer be 'their' hospital for which

---

8 4,228 eggs were donated or purchased in 1925, and in 1930 when the committee complained that the supply received at the last Egg Day in May had 'only lasted till Christmas', the town quickly donated a further 1,000.

they had worked so hard and raised so much money, but it enabled the hospital to survive. In 2006 plans are well advanced for its replacement with a new hospital, care home and health centre on a single site. There was much debate and so much public interest in these plans that meetings were held in the parish church because the town hall could not accommodate the numbers. One of the main concerns was that the hospital should remain within the National Health Service.

Other important developments happened in the educational field. At the beginning of the twentieth century secondary education was almost entirely in private schools and thus available only to those who could afford the fees. St Margaret's School for girls, in a large house at 35 New Street, took boarders at fees ranging from 8 to 15 guineas a term. Day pupils paid £1 11s 6d to £3 3s 0d per term. The prospectus sent out by the Principal, Miss D Miller BA, LRAM, listed an impressive range of subjects taught, or available as extras (from half to three guineas a term), by her staff of 'Certified Resident Mistresses and Professional Visiting Masters and Mistresses'. In addition to the basic subjects there were Latin, French, German, natural science and both theoretical and practical chemistry, needlework and 'drilling' (PE today). Extra subjects were strong on music, including piano, harmony and counterpoint, violin, organ, solo singing and dancing as well as gymnastics, painting, elocution and fancy needlework.

Across the road at the British School, girls and boys were receiving a more basic education in not much more than the 'three Rs' up to the age of about thirteen, and then usually leaving to find work. However, the Education Act of 1902 set up Local Education Authorities with power to provide secondary schools paid for out of the rates, and to offer scholarships to children from elementary schools. There were still fees to pay and uniforms to buy, and for anyone in Chipping Norton who aspired to such an education there was also the need to travel to a school in Banbury, Burford, Oxford or Chipping Campden. This situation did not improve until the building of a new Chipping Norton Grammar School in Burford Road, which opened in 1928 with some 40 pupils and grew steadily thereafter. Children unsuccessful in the '11+' exam for the grammar school were catered for in the former National and British schools, and eventually a 'secondary modern' school in The Green. In the early1960s Oxfordshire adopted the comprehensive principle and the Grammar School was enlarged and opened to all children from a wide catchment area around the town. Local sensitivities meant that it was not until a few years later that it changed its name, dropping the 'Grammar' label and becoming simply Chipping Norton School. St Mary's Church of England

School provided primary schooling from the old school site in The Green. Holy Trinity Roman Catholic Primary School was enlarged and the nuns who originally ran it were eventually succeeded by lay teachers.

In 1904 a branch of the National Children's Homes was opened in New Street, occupying a large building originally built by William Bliss as two imposing 'semi-detached villas' for his son and son-in-law. Renamed Penhurst, it cared for and educated many severely handicapped children and became a significant part of the community of Chipping Norton, its annual fete being a popular occasion attended by many local people and raising considerable sums. In the 1990s the size of the home was reduced, vacating the main building, but keeping the name Penhurst.

The period between the wars was a difficult time for many people, especially in industrial areas which experienced severe unemployment, but the worst effects of inter-war depression were not felt quite so much in Chipping Norton. Oxford was one of the few towns in the country offering well-paid employment in the 1930s, because of its rapidly expanding car industry, and as transport improved it became possible for Chipping Norton men to get jobs there – a trend which greatly increased in the second half of the century. The coming of buses in the 1920s, while bringing more people into the town from the surrounding villages, also made it easier for local people to work and shop further afield. The removal of the monthly livestock market to Banbury possibly led to some loss of trade by local shopkeepers and had the lasting effect of opening up the market place for car parking.

In spite of, or perhaps because of, the hardships of life in the first half of the twentieth century, people in the community were energetic in forming all sorts of clubs and societies and taking part in a wide variety of sports and cultural activities. New clubs were founded for football, hockey, tennis and golf, in addition to the much older cricket club. Undoubtedly the most unusual was the Baseball Club founded in 1920. The game was introduced much earlier around 1910 by Fred Lewis, a local man who became renowned in Chipping Norton for his energy and sense of humour. Three years before, he had started a scout group[9] for young boys and was looking for some activity which they could take part in. Baseball proved so popular that he later started the club which went on to claim the title of England Champions in 1926. It lasted until the 1950s. As leisure time increased in the second half of the century, facilities continued to expand. Football teams for quite young children were organised by groups of parents, the golf club extended its course from 9 to 18

---

9 Possibly one of the first in England.

holes. In the late 1960s the then head of the comprehensive school, Arthur Nockels, replaced football with rugby and this eventually lead to the starting of a town rugby club. Its clubhouse and ground adjoined the bowls club, also started at that time. The town also built its own open-air heated swimming pool, raising much of the money through donations and local fund raising. In the 1990s a much larger indoor pool was provided by the District and County councils as part of a new leisure centre adjoining Chipping Norton School, but enthusiasts for the old open-air pool renamed it 'the Lido' and launched a lively campaign to fund its continued use.

In the late nineteenth century the Salvation Army and the Temperance 'Band of Hope' provided bands to attract support for their organisations, and these were eventually succeeded by the Chipping Norton Silver Band, as well as by a small but very popular 'Bluetones' dance band which regularly played for dances in the Town Hall and elsewhere. In 1973 another Salvation Army band gave a concert at one of the first performances in the new theatre established by Tamara and John Malcolm in the old citadel in Spring Street. The Theatre flourished under Tamara's direction and went on to earn a reputation far beyond Chipping Norton. For many years there were two cinemas, one in London Road and another 'The Regent' which lasted in New Street until replaced by a squash and fitness club of the same name in the 1980s. The Stour Choral Union was formed in the early years of the century and held annual festivals in Chipping Norton for local choirs, which by the end of the century had expanded into a major local occasion for musicians of all kinds. Adult Education also flourished from the 1970s through the Community Education Centre at the Comprehensive School and the work of Oxford University's Department for Continuing Education and the Workers' Education Association.

In 1938 everyone in the town had been issued with a gas mask as another world war approached. This was a war which would affect everyone, even those not called up for active service and living in a small country town like Chipping Norton. A Local Defence Volunteer unit was formed (later the Home Guard) under the command of Colonel Chamberlayne, their duties including guarding the water tower and the railway tunnel as well as Leafield wireless station. Troops were billeted in various buildings around the town, including Hitchman's Brewery and the Baptist Church, and on one occasion men of the Durham Light Infantry were reviewed in the Market Place by King George VI before they marched off in the early hours of a winter morning down to the station, en route for France and ultimately the beaches of Dunkirk from which many did not return. A Friday afternoon in September brought what is reputed to be the longest train ever to come to Chipping Norton, so long that it had to move forward and stop again to allow its passengers to step onto the platform. These were 321 evacuee children clutching gas masks and labels with their names and home addresses, and their 40 teachers and other adult helpers from West Ham in London. Taken to the Regent Cinema and the Baptist schoolroom under the direction of the local Red Cross and St John's Ambulance Brigade, they were given food parcels to last the first forty-eight hours and allocated to their new homes with local families by 7.30 that evening. A further 500 arrived the next day to be billeted in surrounding villages. Some did not stay long, being taken home by their parents before Christmas, but many were here for much longer, perhaps for two or three years. These were not the only evacuees who sought shelter in Chipping Norton during the war and the Town Clerk, Frank Morris, was constantly involved in dealing with the effects of the government's evacuation schemes, replying to directives and surveys, dealing with the inevitable tensions and complaints from house-holders about the people billeted on them and trying to sort out innumerable administrative matters. The main group of children evacuated to Chipping Norton came from the New City Road School in West Ham, and in order to cope with so many extra children local schools operated a shift system, local children in the mornings and evacuees in the afternoons, and extra space was found in the old Baptist school-

Evacuee children from London arriving at Chipping Norton in 1939 at the outbreak of war. (Chipping Norton Museum)

room.[10] Another problem was the difficulty of feeding the children at lunchtime and the 'British Restaurant' run by members of the WRVS helped with this.

The situation became worse towards the end of 1940. In one of many replies sent by Morris to people wanting emergency accommodation he wrote 'We have filled every available space and I am sorry I cannot help you ... We have had for weeks coachloads of women and children from West Ham and that district ... the army requisitions have finished any possibility of assisting and much as we are willing our position is now hopeless.' By June 1940 a thousand soldiers and airmen were billeted in Chipping Norton. As well as these men a number of their wives and families sought accommodation here, as did many others whose homes had been destroyed in the blitz. In July 1940 even the former workhouse, now called a Public Assistance Institution, was taken over by the Ministry of Health as an emergency hospital 'for military sick and civilian casualties'. When the government sent notice that they were drawing up contingency plans for a further 200 children to be evacuated to Chipping Norton, the despairing Town Clerk replied that it was impossible to take any more, pointing out that the water and sanitation system in the town was already inadequate to meet the needs of the numbers living here.

Later came the German air attacks and the drone of enemy planes heading for Coventry, Birmingham and other large towns, and the local volunteer fire brigade was called out to support firemen in distant places. Chipping Norton did not suffer any damage from bombing being far from the major targets, but there were designated public air-raid shelters under the Regent Cinema and in the cellars of the brewery.[11] A Wellington bomber returning to base early one morning after a night raid over Germany crashed in Church Street after colliding with another British plane on a training exercise. The crew of the Wellington all died. The entry of America into the war brought American troops into the town and neighbourhood in October 1943, some of whom

---

10 Molly Fuller and Stanley Wykes came as teachers from the New City Road School and stayed with their pupils. When they eventually returned to London they married and Stanley was called up, but after the war they came back to settle in Chipping Norton, becoming well known and popular members of the local community. Stanley Wykes became head of St Mary's School and was Mayor in 1957.

11 Even the medieval cellar under 20 High Street provided shelter for one mother and daughter who spent a whole morning in it because they did not hear the 'all-clear' siren.

were housed at the brewery for several weeks. The chestnut trees in New Street sheltered heavy tanks before D-Day.

Everyone learned to cope with food rationing. There were 'Union Jack' and 'British' restaurants to supply cheap hot meals for people doing war work in the town. The iron railings round the churchyard and Penhurst were taken away, supposedly for melting down to make tanks and aeroplanes. The Hub Iron Works worked three consecutive shifts covering 24 hours and women were employed there for the first time. Nearly £750,000 was raised by local people for the war effort, a considerable sum for a small community. It included money raised to 'adopt' two destroyers, HMS Heythrop and HMS Magpie. At Greystones on the Burford Road a prison camp was set up for German and Italian prisoners of war. About 450 men were housed there in huts and were employed on local farms, road repairs or other jobs. One of them, a German prisoner called Conrad Gries, drew sketches of the town, and one of his drawings hangs in the Town Hall today.[12]

Hundreds of men from Chipping Norton were among those called up to the forces, and inevitably some did not return. Their names were added to the list on the memorial in the church and a new public war memorial was erected at the bottom of Rock Hill, where the Armistice Day commemoration continues to be held each year. A new memorial plaque recording those from the village was also erected on the front of what is now Gert's Cottage in Over Norton.

Some of the old firms which had provided employment and contributed to the prosperity of the town for many years began to decline towards the end of the century. Still trading under the name of Bliss, the tweed mill now owned by Fox Brothers continued as the town's main employer until it finally closed in 1980, due to the contraction of the textile industry nationally. Although it was said that this mill's order books were still full, the parent company needed to economise and so concentrated all work at its Wellington mill. The news was a great shock to Chipping Norton not only for those who lost their jobs. The fine Victorian mill was protected from demolition by 'listing' and some years later was successfully converted into apartments. Fortunately a newer

---

12 Gries was a young soldier stationed in the Channel Islands with the German occupying forces. Ordered to make a map showing where they had laid mines around the islands, he secretly made a second copy which he hid in the hope that the allies would find it. His story is recorded in the Alderney Museum. A couple from Chipping Norton met him by chance many years later while on holiday in Scotland in the 1980s.

business was expanding at this time at the other end of the town. Parker Knoll, the High Wycombe furniture makers, had opened a small branch in the London Road in 1962, but in the 1970s transferred most of their business, especially the upholstery side, to Chipping Norton. Their continued expansion helped to alleviate the loss of Bliss's, but in 2005 even they were forced to close because of changing markets and economic circumstances.

Hitchman's Brewery had already ceased brewing beer in 1932 but continued to make mineral water and trade in wines and spirits until 1970. The Hub Iron Works lasted a decade longer. This small firm had grown out of a nineteenth-century ironmonger's business owned by Robert Rowell, probably undertaking some manufacturing alongside the rest of his expanding business. His descendants Norman and Jack Rowell formed the Hub Ironworks Ltd in 1920. The foundry was in Albion Street, where a lucrative trade was established casting, among other things, traffic signs, street names and guide posts for the rapidly developing road system throughout Oxfordshire and elsewhere. Like others, the Hub converted its output to war work in 1939. After the war the firm survived successfully until the general decline in British manufacturing industry in the late 1970s, and finally closed in 1982. The loss of these firms was to some extent compensated for by new businesses coming into the town. It was the policy of both town and district councils to encourage this by providing new industrial estates with appropriate light industrial units. While many inhabitants travelled to work in other places, Chipping Norton managed to avoid becoming merely a dormitory.

The councils themselves had been re-organised. One of the most significant changes in Chipping Norton in the twentieth century was brought about by the Local Government Act which abolished its borough status in 1974. As part of a reorganisation of local government throughout Britain, the Borough Council was downgraded to the status of a parish and most of its former powers transferred to a new District Council covering an area called West Oxfordshire, with headquarters in Witney. As a former borough its only distinction was to be called a 'Town' rather than Parish council, and to be able to appoint a Town Mayor instead of a chairman. The change increased the financial resources and range of professional expertise available through the enlarged District, but undoubtedly reduced the democratic involvement of the inhabitants, who became less directly responsible for running their own town. The sixteen councillors of the Borough had been local residents, well known to and easily lobbied by local people, and elections always attracted plenty of candidates and a high turn-out of voters (with results announced after the count late at night to an eager crowd waiting on the Town Hall steps). After

1974 interest in the Town Council inevitably declined because it had few powers and only limited resources and it was sometimes difficult to attract candidates. Chipping Norton was allotted three representatives on the West Oxfordshire District Council, who could do little more than attempt to influence the decisions of the majority.

Among the powers exercised by the old Borough had been that of providing housing for rent by people unable to afford the cost of buying, and several hundred houses, flats and bungalows were built by the council, the earliest ones in the 1920s, but most between 1940 and 1974. Some of these replaced older substandard houses which were overcrowded and lacked modern facilities but the majority were additions to the stock of houses available in the town. Families welcomed the much more comfortable homes and there were always waiting lists. The new houses were built mainly on the southern side of the town, between Churchill Road and Walterbush Road. This area, known at first as the 'Hailey Fields Estate', had once been farmland, part of it belonging to the chapel at Hailey near Witney.[13] It was later occupied by allotments and eventually purchased by the council in the 1940s. At the end of the war when there was a severe housing shortage, a number of 'prefabs' were built here, which although only intended as a temporary expedient, lasted for about thirty years. When the District Council became the housing authority in 1974 it completed Cornish Road and later developed another area around Dunstan Avenue between New Street and The Leys. These large estates, together with private developments in other areas, greatly increased the extent of the town.

Beneficial changes also affected the workhouse. Ever since the introduction of old age pensions in 1908 the number of people unable to support themselves had been declining nationally and more humane ways of helping people in the community were being adopted. There were gradual relaxations of the regime and better care for the sick and mentally handicapped who made up the majority of inmates. In 1948 Chipping Norton's former workhouse became Cotshill Hospital for the Mentally Handicapped. It was finally closed in the 1980s and remaining patients either transferred elsewhere or housed in supervised accommodation in the town. The grim building was sold and converted into attractive apartments (to the amazement of many local people who remembered its past). New private houses were built within its grounds

---

13 William Wright of Over Norton left £100 to the poor of the parish of Hailey in 1786. They invested the capital in fifty acres of land in Chipping Norton and used the income for the benefit of their poor.

and the high wall which had once confined the inmates now provided a sense of security for the new occupants.

In 1962 the last trains ran from Chipping Norton and the railway was closed as part of a reduction of the national rail network recommended by the 'Beeching plan'. Such small stations and branch lines were deemed unprofitable. The decline of railways has been more than matched by the growth of road transport for both people and goods. By 1969 the main road passing right through the centre of the town was becoming increasingly crowded with traffic. The narrowness of this road at the top of New Street made it quite unsuitable for large lorries and buses which had to mount the equally narrow pavements in order to pass each other on this stretch, and some action to improve this situation was urgently needed. A disastrous decision was made not to divert the traffic but to widen the bottleneck by demolishing a whole row of shops in the narrow section of New Street and several other buildings on the lower side of Market Place, including Webb's department store and the seventeenth-century Unicorn Inn. In spite of strong opposition, particularly from the Council for the Protection of Rural England and some local inhabitants, the majority of the Borough Council supported the proposal of the highway authority on the somewhat doubtful grounds that the town would die if traffic was deterred from coming through it, and the road widening went ahead. Inevitably the result was that even more traffic was encouraged to come through the centre of Chipping Norton, causing increasing noise and pollution particularly from very large lorries which seriously reduced the attractiveness of the town centre and contributed nothing to its economy. The irony of history is that the very roads which gave Chipping Norton an advantage as a market in its early days had now become its biggest problem.

For nearly fifty years, from 1869 until 1928, the main newspaper serving the north of the county was the *Oxfordshire Weekly News* edition published from Chipping Norton. It carried detailed accounts of a range of local activities as well as county and occasionally national news in dense columns of small print. It was succeeded a few years later by the *Chipping Norton Advertiser* which lasted until 1970. These papers kept people informed of some at least of the happenings in their town, but when the *Advertiser* was taken over by the *Banbury Guardian* it carried less and less news from Chipping Norton and finally ceased publication. In 1976 a public meeting was held in the Town Hall which lead to the foundation of a new community-based newspaper run by a small group of local people, lead by a former head of St Mary's Primary School and a retired *Times* correspondent. The *Chipping Norton News* produced its first issue in December 1976 and became an important and popular aspect of the life of the town, as it still is thirty years later, achieving a high standard of reporting and presentation, giving local people a voice and helping to preserve a sense of community which other developments might have weakened.

By the end of the twentieth century Chipping Norton, like other towns, had experienced not only greater changes than in any previous century, but also a much faster pace of change. The population was just under 6,000, an increase of more than 50% in a century. Although the traditional open-air market itself has shrunk considerably, Chipping Norton still functions as a market town providing a range of shops, services and employment to its inhabitants and to those in surrounding villages. Growth has been much faster, however, in Banbury, Witney and other towns to which access is now very easy by car. Most of the changes have been brought about by influences beyond local control, through central government policies, economic circumstances, developments in transport, etc., and they continually challenge the inhabitants to adapt and find new ways to preserve and promote Chipping Norton's individual identity.

Bibliography

CNMus = Chipping Norton Museum.
P = privately printed. Copies can often be found in the Chipping Norton Museum.

A Ballard, *Notes on the History of Chipping Norton,* 1893, Reprinted by
    CNMus
M Bee & P Tyrrell, *The Chipping Norton Co-operative Society 1866–1968,*
    CNMus 2000
J Blair, *Anglo-Saxon Oxfordshire,* 1994 Alan Sutton Publishing
P Booth ,*The Romans in North-West Oxfordshire* In J Howells (ed.) *The*
    Chipping Norton Area, Chipping Norton Museum, 2001
M Breakell, *The Twentieth Century and Beyond* in J Howells (ed.) *The*
    Chipping Norton Area Chipping Norton Museum 2001
Brasenose College Quartercentenary Monographs
W Burson, *Jog Trot Days: Chipping Norton in the 1920s.* Bodkin Books.
G N Clark & G D H Cole, *The Strike at Chipping Norton* Oxon Record
    Office, GAOxon c317
Chipping Norton Local History Society and Chipping Norton Museum
    Chipping Norton in Old Photographs, 1987 – and several further volumes
        based on the extensive collection of photographs in the museum
D Eddershaw*, The Civil War in Oxfordshire,* Alan Sutton Publishing, 1995
    Chipping Norton Street Names, The Bookshop Chipping Norton, 1999
    Chipping Norton & District Hospital 1920–1970 (P)
    The Chipping Norton Area 1600–1900 in J Howells (ed), *The Chipping*
        Norton Area, CNMus 2001
    Roman Finds at Chipping Norton in Oxoniensia vol xxxvii, 1972
    The Riot of 1845 and the Policing of Chipping Norton in *Top Oxon* 1974.
        Oxfordshire Local History Association
R. Ll. Evans, *The Bliss Mills and the Bliss Family in Chipping Norton* and
    Dunstan House, Penhurst and the Upper Bliss Mill. Both in *Top.Oxon.,* nos.
    20 and 21, Oxfordshire Local History Association
A Fletcher & D McCulloch, *Tudor Rebellions*, Longmans, 5th ed. 2004
J Foster, *Alumni Oxonienses 1500–1714,* Parker, Oxford and London 1891–92

J Grantham, *The Regulated Pasture: Common Land in Chipping Norton,* 1997 (P)

J H Harvey, *The Perpendicular Style 1330–1485,* Batsford, London 1978

M Henig & P Booth, *Roman Oxfordshire,* Sutton Publishing, 2000

J.R.Hodgkins, *Over the Hills to Glory, Radicalism in Banburyshire 1832–1945,* Chapter 11 *The Bliss Tweed Mill Strike 1913–14,* Clifton Press 1978

J Howells (ed.), *The Chipping Norton Area: a series of lectures on the changing landscape of North West Oxfordshire,* CNMus, 2001

H Hurrell , *The Bliss Mill,* 1996 (P)

The Hub Ironworks, 2001 (P)

A Jones, *Commotion Time: the English Risings of 1549,* unpublished thesis, Warwick University 2003

C Kirtland, *Brief Memorials of the Early History of Chipping Norton,* 1871

G Lambrick, *The Rollright Stones,* 1983 Oxford Archaeological Unit

D Lewis (revised R Mann and P Watkins), *Chipping Norton Inns,* CNMus 2004

R Mann, *Some Episodes in the History of St Mary's parish church,* 2002 (P)

An Eminent Puritan, the life & times of Edmund Hall, 2003 (P)

Edward Stone & the discovery of aspirin, 2003 (P)

Chipping Norton Fair, 2004 (P)

E Meades, *The History of Chipping Norton,* 2nd edition 1984, Bodkin Bookshop.

O Meades, *The Adventures of Captain James Hind of Chipping Norton.* 1985 (P)

N Millea, *The Oldest Maps of Chipping Norton* in J Howells (ed) *The Chipping Norton Area,* CNMus, 2001

Oxford Dictionary of National Biography, OUP, 2004

Oxfordshire Record Society, *Journals*

Newspapers: *The Chipping Norton News, Jackson's Oxford Journal, Oxfordshire Weekly News,* and other local newspapers held at the Centre for Oxfordshire Studies.

M Pearson, *Chipping Norton in Bygone Days,* 1909

Rawlinson, *Parochial Collections*

K Rodwell (ed.), *Historic Towns of Oxfordshire,* 1975

J Steane, *North-West Oxfordshire in the Middle Ages* in J Howells (ed) *The Chipping Norton Area* CNMus,2001

The Victoria County History of Oxfordshire

Willan, *History of the Oxfordshire Regiment of Militia,* 1900

Original sources

Acts of the Privy Council

Calendar of Close Rolls

Calendar of Fine Rolls

Calendar of Hundred Rolls
Calendar of Patent Rolls
Calendar of State Papers
Census Returns 1841–1901
Chancery Records
Chipping Norton and Salford Enclosure Award, 1770
Chipping Norton Charter of Incorporation, 1607
Dean and Chapter of Gloucester Records
Deeds and other records held in Chipping Norton Museum
Exchequer Records
Letters and Papers of Henry VIII
Minute Books of the Bailiffs and Burgesses, 1720–1835
Oxfordshire Domesday Book
Parish Registers for Chipping Norton
PCC Probate Records
Probate Records for Chipping Norton in the Oxfordshire Record Office
Records of the Churchwardens and Overseers of the Poor for Chipping
     Norton
Report of the Commissioners for the Enquiry Concerning Charities, 1825
Report of the Commissioners on the Municipal Corporations of England and
     Wales, 1835
Star Chamber Records
The Case of the Bailiffs and Burgesses of Chipping Norton 1769
Valor Ecclesiasticus, 1535
Worcester Priory Accounts

Index